# The
# Best
# Best Man

Othe titles in the Wedding Collection

# The Best Best Man

by
Jacqueline Eames

## foulsham
LONDON • NEW YORK • TORONTO • SYDNEY

# foulsham
Bennetts Close, Cippenham, Berkshire SL1 5AP

While every effort has been made to ensure
the accuracy of all the information contained
within this book, neither the author nor the
publisher can be liable for any errors. In
particular, since laws change from time to
time, it is vital that each individual checks
relevant legal details for themselves.

ISBN 0-572-02339-1

Editor: Carole Chapman

Photoset in Great Britain by Encounter Photosetting, Fleet, Hants.
Printed in Great Britain by Cox & Wyman Ltd, Reading, Berks.

# Contents

# *Foreword*

A popular misconception about the best man is that he is chosen for his role at the wedding on account of his colourful wit and glowing qualities. Nearer the truth of the matter is the fact that a best man is a normal human being. He often has little idea about wedding organisation and probably bites his nails at the prospect of making a speech. He accepts the responsibilities of the post, because the groom, perhaps a lifelong friend, has asked this favour of him and he could not refuse.

This book presents the best man with a guide to all the technical details of a wedding from transport to attire. He will see all the likely points of mishap and learn how to avoid them. He will realise that the most daunting prospect facing the best man – the wedding speech – can easily be overcome even without the talent and wit of a natural comedian.

On rare occasions, there may be a female 'best man' needing all of this information. However, since the best man is traditionally the groom's closest friend, it is unlikely, even in these days of advancing equality, that this will happen often. The bride may have reason to think she should occupy that place, after all! There have been female 'best men' and there will be more but since they will be only too aware of their unusual position, I am sure they will forgive the use of the male pronoun throughout this book. Apart from obvious matters such as helping the groom to dress, her own attire and choice of dancing partners, a female best man will conduct herself in much the same way as a best man.

# ·1·
# Before the Day

£279

# ·1·
# The Appointment

The custom of the bride and groom surrounding themselves with a wedding party originates from the days when the bride was captured from her family. The groom took a group of supporters with him to distract the bride's family while he whisked her away. Once the bride had been successfully captured, he sent his 'best man' to soothe her family's tempers!

Today, special attendants act as helpers in all sorts of capacities. For the bride, her attendants are her chief bridesmaid and other bridesmaids; the groom chooses a best man and ushers. The number of attendants is a matter for the bride and groom to decide. Every wedding requires two witnesses, but it may be preferred that the parents fulfil this role.

It is customary for the best man to be a bachelor, but a groom who prefers to ask a married friend to act as his supporter is quite at liberty to do so. Indeed, some people believe that a married man remembering his own experiences and needs can give better service to the groom.

'To qualify for the post of best man the successful applicant will be sober, level-headed, punctual, thorough, of harmonious disposition, tactful, witty and decisive.'

If you can fulfil all these qualifications your friend

11

the groom will be lucky indeed to have such a model of perfection as his mentor!

These are the ideal qualities for the best man, but in reality it is extremely rare to find them all in one person. Very few people are born to be superb best men and yet people are doing a great job every day. To be honest, most best men are selected on the strength of a lifelong friendship and usually for no other reason.

The role of the best man is to assist the groom before and at the wedding. He reassures the groom when he is nervous and is there to give support and help whenever needed. He is an organiser and should be relied upon to handle details such as ensuring that the ushers are in the right place at the right time and are correctly dressed. Successful best-man-ship is attained by the assimilation of facts about the wedding day and the ability to act as liaison officer between a large number of people and the source of information – the bride herself.

Basically the best man's major duties are as follows:

1 Helping the groom to choose the ushers and to explain their duties for the wedding day.
2 Helping the groom to organise the stag party and to see that he arrives home afterwards without mishap.
3 Getting the groom to the church on time.
4 Handing the ring over to the groom at the appropriate moment in the ceremony.
5 Organising transport for the guests from the church to the reception.
6 Making a speech at the wedding reception.
7 Seeing that the couple leave the reception on time.

On paper it all sounds easy, but to do the job properly, to be in command of the situation, to see that everything runs smoothly, you will have to know every detail of the wedding arrangements, backwards, forwards, and sideways. There are rarely disasters at a wedding, but if there are snags – all eyes turn to the best man to solve the problems. Be sure you know all the likely points of mishap, well before the wedding day. Preparation is the key to acquiring all the qualities and performing all the duties of the perfect best man.

## · QUALITIES ·

### Sobriety
Maintaining a clear head amid the euphoria of the wedding celebrations is vital for the best man. Although taxis or lifts are essential for the stag party, you should be sober enough to see the groom to his front door afterwards. You should remain sober on the wedding eve, so that the next day is not spent fighting a hangover and you must remain sober enough at the wedding reception to deliver an articulate speech and to see the couple off the premises at the right time.

### Common Sense
An element of common sense will help you through most problems, should any arise on the day. However, if this does not happen to be your strong point, a few sensible precautions can be taken. Being on good terms with the chief bridesmaid and the bride's and groom's fathers will prove to be a big help should their assistance be necessary. One

wonders how often, if ever, that joke situation of the wedding ring falling down a grating in the church has happened. It could happen of course and if you want to take all adequate precautions – buy a substitute gold-coloured band just in case. No one can be absolutely sure how they are going to react in an emergency, but if you are prepared for the more obvious mishaps, such as making a list of taxi firms in your area, in case the car breaks down on the way to church – your nerves will be in better shape on the wedding day.

## Punctuality

It should go without saying that, as you are responsible for the groom's timekeeping, this is a vital quality. If the wedding is to be held early in the day and you know that almost nothing short of a time bomb will get you out of bed, then arrange for a telephone alarm call and once you are up, stay up. If you do not have a telephone, ask an understanding neighbour to bang on the door until you answer. At a registry office wedding good time keeping is essential since there is usually a string of weddings throughout the day at about twenty-minute intervals. If one couple is late, they may have to miss their turn altogether.

## Thoroughness

Although the responsibilities of organising a wedding fall largely on the bride's family, you must inform yourself about all the details, even though many of them may not seem to be any direct concern of yours. It is often suggested that the groom should liaise closely with the chief bridesmaid, but there could be a snag here. For

14

example, there may not be a bridesmaid; or she may live at John O'Groats, when the wedding is to be held at Land's End; or the eldest attendant may be no more than six. The one person who knows everything there is to know about the wedding is the bride herself.

It is necessary to know the format for the day, what to expect, where to be and at what time, and all the duties involved. The size of the bride's family may make a difference to the best man's role. If she has plenty of brothers and sisters to help with the organising, the best man may find that he is relieved of many jobs. You should not be left to make vague guesses as to what is required – the bride and groom should inform you of as much as possible and well in advance. It is important for the best man to meet with the bride and groom and also the chief bridesmaid if possible as arrangements take shape.

## Communication Skills

The best man has to communicate with people of all ages and stations at the wedding, from the smallest bridesmaid to the oldest grandmother. It is part of your job to be charming to everyone. This could include appearing to be enthralled by the never-ending reminiscences about the bride's childhood from a doting aunt and then switching your attention to the page boy's chocolate-covered fingers before he makes a grab at the bride's veil. It goes without saying that you must look as though you are enjoying every minute.

## Observation and Tact

You will be expected to see that the reception runs smoothly. Keep an eye open for dry corners and let the waiters know about people who seem to be overlooked. You might have to disengage the bride and groom from people who seem to be monopolising their company – there is always one notorious bore at every wedding. If the vicar has decreed that no confetti should be thrown in the church grounds, make sure that people are informed and comply. Check to see whether the vicar will allow photographs to be taken in church – if he will not, detail the ushers to warn people with cameras as they enter the church.

## A Good Speaker

The speech is probably the moment that the best man dreads the most. A good speech is important but no one expects a polished, witty professional performance. Three to four minutes is ample; the best speeches are always the shortest ones and with a little preparation and practice, success should be achieved.

Very few people are possessed with the art of being witty and if you as the best man are not, then forget about trying to learn how to be the world's greatest wit before the wedding day – it simply will not work. Just concentrate on being sincere in your wedding speech and remember that most people are too busy talking and eating to be over-critical about what you say unless you waffle on for too long.

# THE APPOINTMENT

It is a great honour to be asked to be best man; a vote of the groom's friendship and confidence but the groom must consider that the job should give his friend pleasure and that it is not everyone who relishes the responsibility. His friend has no obligation to accept the honour, especially if he is the shy retiring type.

# · 2 ·
# *Preliminaries*

Your role as the best man begins from the moment you have been selected by the prospective groom and have agreed to undertake the responsibility. Though you are not officially involved in the wedding preparations, you need to have a good working knowledge of the arrangements so that you can discharge your duties properly, leaving the chief participants free to relax and enjoy the day. Ideally, the best man should be in on discussions of wedding plans from the start.

As far as the bride's family is concerned preparations for the wedding will begin as soon as the engagement is announced formally, either in the newspaper, by means of a celebratory party, or simply by word of mouth. Six months is generally the accepted length of time to allow for detailed planning, although these days some churches and reception premises have to be booked many months in advance, particularly for a Saturday wedding. The bride and groom should allow ample time to discuss their arrangements with you so that you are clear about what is expected. You should not be left guessing.

## · **PRIORITY TALKS** ·

If the attendants at the wedding include an adult bridesmaid, ask the groom to arrange a meeting between himself, the bride, the bridesmaid and yourself, so that you can discuss exactly what everyone will have to do before the wedding day. If, as we have already discussed, there are no bridesmaids – go ahead with the meeting anyway and get all the details from the bride herself.

At this stage you will need to know the following facts:

1 The venue for the wedding ceremony
2 The date of the wedding
3 The time of the wedding
4 The venue and type of reception: a full wedding breakfast, buffet or other

If the bride and groom both live locally it is likely that you will know of the church and reception premises, but nevertheless you could take a drive from the groom's home to the church and then on to the reception venue to see exactly how long it takes and, most important, to find out what car parking facilities there are at both the church and reception grounds.

The number of guests is an important factor because it will determine the number of ushers required on the day, and the type of reception will determine some of the finer points of your duties.

## · THE INVITATIONS ·

Ideally the invitations should go out from the bride's home at least six weeks before the wedding.

Although the best man and other attendants will already have been consulted, they will also receive invitations to which they should reply briefly, formally and immediately within three days of receipt. Formal replies should be composed in the third person, for instance:

> *Tom Tate accepts with pleasure Mr and Mrs North's kind invitation to the marriage of their daughter, Nel, to Sam South at ... on ... at ... and afterwards at ... .*

or:

> *Tom Tate thanks Mr and Mrs North for their kind invitation and will be delighted to accept.*

There is no need to add your signature to your reply.

## · THE USHERS ·

The ushers are the best man's team of helpers for whom he is responsible. Traditionally, they are unmarried and are usually brothers or close relatives of the bride and groom. Generally, there are as many ushers as there are bridesmaids so that they may escort the bridesmaids during the course of the day.

Selection of the ushers should be made by the

groom with helpful hints thrown in by the best man about the suitability of choice. It is sensible to choose those who do not have to face a long journey on the day and better still if they have their own transport.

The ushers should be kept aware of all the arrangements and details so that one of them could take over from you at a moment's notice, should the need arise. It is the best man who is responsible for seeing that all ushers deal with their assigned duties. It creates a much more friendly atmosphere on the wedding day if the principal men have met. They will probably meet again at the stag night but this is obviously not the time for talking about wedding details!

Ushers should be responsible, level-headed people chosen for their friendliness, dignity and unflappability, not the sort who are likely to adjourn to the nearest bar for a quick drink before the service leaving early guests to fend for themselves, but if their responsibilities extend to a pregnant wife with small children, or a lengthy journey from one end of the country to the other to attend the wedding, it might be better to make another choice.

For a wedding of about a hundred people there should be four ushers; one for every twenty five guests.

The duties of an usher are not onerous but if the job is done well, it helps the smooth running of the day and takes care of several minor worries of those principally involved in the organising. The best man ensures that they know and carry out their duties:

1  One will give out service sheets at the church door.

2 One will stand at the foot of the aisle to ask on which side of the church the guests wish to sit (bride's family and friends on the left; groom's on the right).

3 Another will stand half way down the aisle to usher people to their seats.

4 The fourth, the chief usher, will be posted at the church door to escort the bride's mother to her seat on arrival at the church.

If the wedding is to be a very large affair there may be a fifth usher to direct people to car parks.

The benefit of service sheets is that the congregation can follow the service and the hymns without referring back and forth from prayer book to hymn book. They also eliminate the need to share church books. On the wedding day the groom holds two copies and passes one to the bride inside the church. Bridesmaids acquire their copies from pew ends when they reach the chancel steps. The best man should collect the sheets in advance from the bride's mother and pass them on to the chief usher who ensures that one of the other ushers distributes them to the people as they enter church.

Ushers must arrive early at the church to distribute the order of service sheets and buttonholes and show guests to their seats. Punctuality is as vital for the ushers as it is for the best man for there is nothing worse than a late arrival panting down the aisle seconds before the bridal procession is due to start. It looks bad and upsets everyone else's careful planning. If one of the nominated ushers is notoriously late for everything do find someone else.

After the wedding ceremony the ushers should

help to organise transport for the guests from the church to the reception and the best man may ask one to remain behind to check for any property left in the church.

At the reception they escort the bridesmaids and keep an eye on the food and drinks situation to see that there are no dry corners. They do not form part of the receiving line, but should mingle with guests.

## · TRANSPORT ·

The best man is responsible for getting the groom and himself to the church on time and should take charge of the arrangements for getting the other guests safely dispatched to the reception – not forgetting himself! It is customary for the best man to arrange for a car to take the newly-weds on the first stage of their honeymoon.

Although there are no strict rules concerning responsibility for transport costs, some families divide the cost of cars, the bride's parents paying for the cars that take the wedding party to church and the groom for the return journey. This is obviously a matter for delicate negotiation and in this, as in all other matters of wedding finance, the best man may be relied upon to be both go-between and fixer.

If the best man uses his own car, he must check beforehand that it is in good working order ready for the wedding day. In order to be suitably prepared and as sure as possible about the timetable, he should do a couple of test runs before the day, at the right time and on the relevant day of the week to ascertain the time it will take. Traffic conditions will need checking and anything unusual, for instance roadworks and special events such as a carnival! Parking arrangements at the church and reception venue will also need to be checked in advance.

Since the advent of the package-deal holiday, honeymoons abroad have become very popular and the first night is often spent at the new home or at a hotel until the flight is ready to leave. It is most unlikely that the couple will use their own car to leave the reception and it would be unreasonable to expect the best man to do the driving, so more usually a hire car or taxi is arranged and in advance. The bride and groom should inform the best man of the time they intend to leave the reception so that he is able to make suitable arrangements. It is the best man who should ensure that the going-away transport is safely parked and available after the reception. If the best man hires cars, he should do this well in advance and double check arrangements a day or so before the wedding day. He will also need to know when the car is being delivered or whether it should be collected, the deadlines imposed and the charges.

If one can ever make a generalisation about the qualifications of the best man, the ability to drive must rank high on the list. While this is not an essential, a best man with his own transport can be a godsend during the preparations and in an emergency. It is a wise precaution to make sure that if the best man does not drive, one of the ushers can.

Regardless of arrangements, it is sensible to have a few reserve cars on stand-by in case of emergencies.

PRELIMINARIES

## The Official Cars
Find out how many official cars are ordered for the wedding day. Depending on the number of attendants there are usually two for the journey from the bride's home to the church and three from the church to the reception.

*To church:*
1  One car is needed for the bride and her father.
2  One car is needed for the bride's mother and the attendants.

*To reception:*
1  One car for the bride and groom.
2  One car for the attendants.
3  One car for the parents of the bride and groom.

## The Guests
There are no specific rules concerning the responsibility for transport except that everyone must be transported safely and that no one should be left behind. The choice of transport is therefore a matter of personal choice but using hire cars or taxis does have the advantage that everyone has the opportunity to enjoy themselves fully without having to worry about driving.

Study the guest list with the bride and groom and tick off all the people who have transport for the wedding and then make a list of all the people who will need a lift. Try to fit everyone in somewhere.

Arriving at the wedding should be the responsibility of each guest who has replied to the invitation, but if the church is a great distance away from the nearest main line station, some people would no doubt welcome a lift to the church. Try to find out exactly who this applies to and detail a few reliable friends to do a shuttle service from the station to the church or organise the services of a taxi firm. It is important that everyone knows in advance who they will transport or who will be responsible for transporting them.

## · RECEPTION VENUE ·

Before the wedding day draws too close, you should try to visit the reception premises with the bride and groom. The bride is bound to want to see the manager to discuss arrangements concerning the menu, the number of guests, the cake, flowers, etc. Take the opportunity to hear what is being said and so furnish yourself with more facts. You can then ask the manager about the general procedure for receptions at the particular venue. He may tell you that you must vacate the premises by a certain time because of a subsequent event. A member of staff may act as toastmaster for the occasion and it will make your life easier on the day of the wedding if you can meet the toastmaster before the occasion and discuss the sequence of speeches and work out a rough timetable. You will probably have to refresh his memory on the wedding day but at least the facts will be in your own mind. Take a look at the likely changing rooms which will be allocated to the bride and groom for the afternoon and see what the car parking facilities are like.

If the venue cannot provide a toastmaster for the occasion, then the speeches, with the exception of your own, and perhaps the guests, will have to be announced by you.

# · 3 ·
# *Attire*

What to wear at the wedding will be your next major point of discussion. You must get the bride's own views about this – don't rely on the groom for he may not agree with what she says and you may be needed to mediate.

The idea of having attendants at the wedding originated with the belief that evil spirits, envious of the couple's happiness, would harm them, but would be confused by the presence of so many similarly dressed people!

Consequently, the principal men, i.e. the groom, the best man, the fathers of the bride and groom and the ushers all dress with the same degree of formality and indeed they may all wear exactly the same or the groom may elect to be slightly different in some way. So, if the groom wears morning suit the other principal members should do the same. If the groom and best man simply wear smart suits, that too will set the scene for other principal men. Strictly speaking, if the bride wears white, the groom and other principal men should wear morning suits.

The best man is normally responsible for the cost of his own wedding clothes. Although there are no hard and fast rules about who should pay for what at the wedding, and nowadays the generally accepted procedure is that attendants pay for their own clothes, strictly speaking this should not apply to additional items in the men's dress.

The groom should consult the principal men and advise them to choose something compatible with his choice and which does not in any way outshine him! If the best man wears brown or maroon when everyone else is dressed in grey, he will be the one who stands out rather than the groom which would be very impolite and photographs will look extremely odd. It can be wise for the groom and best man to shop together as each can act as a useful provider of second opinions. Another consideration is that the colour of the suits and accessories should complement the attire of the female members of the wedding party.

No matter what the choice of attire, it is important to be comfortable, look smart and feel good in a suit that fits.

## · FORMAL DRESS ·

If the wedding is to be a very formal affair, the words 'Morning Dress' can appear on the wedding invitation under the RSVP, but this is not general practice and the bride's wishes are usually spread by word of mouth.

Buying a morning suit is a very expensive business, but if you are going to use this opportunity then buy a suit at one of the better department stores. It may not be cheap, but it should last for a considerable time. All the accessories: shirt, grey topper, grey gloves, can be bought as well. You can use a grey tie for a wedding, but never a black one. Black shoes and socks are the best choice with grey morning suit. If you plan to lead a bright social life with trips to Ascot every year it is probably worth buying the accessories.

Traditional morning suits are three-piece and consist of black coat, grey pin-striped trousers, grey waistcoat, grey tie, grey topper, white shirt, black socks and shoes. For weddings, a grey coat with tails is often substituted and sometimes a cravat is worn instead of a tie. There is no reason why you should not choose some other colour for your morning suit as long as this complements the overall colour scheme of the wedding party. Dark blue, lovat green, wine or brown are all quite acceptable providing that the wearer has the bearing and confidence to carry off the unusual. As a general rule, dark colours are worn for winter and afternoon weddings, lighter colours for summer and morning weddings.

Toppers are removed when entering church and are carried by the brim together with the gloves in the left hand, leaving the right one free for shaking hands. When the groom approaches the chancel steps he leaves his hat and gloves in the pew. Accessories such as the toppers and gloves can be a nuisance at the wedding because you can only wear them for the photographs. They are perhaps too tall to be worn in the car and most of the time is spent carrying them – or leaving them in the church porch to get mixed up with those belonging to others. Although some grooms decide to dispense with them altogether for such reasons, they are an essential part of morning dress.

The cravat is an option to modern morning dress and should always be worn with a high winged collar. The colour of the cravat is purely a matter of personal preference, but the following guide may give you some ideas about ways to tone the accessories to the basic colour of the suit.

| Suit | Shirt | Waistcoat | Tie/Cravat/ Stock | Shoes/ Socks |
|---|---|---|---|---|
| Black | White | Grey/ Cream | Grey/Cream | Black |
| Grey | Blue | Grey | Blue/Grey | Black |
| Brown | Cream | Cream/ Brown | Cream/Brown | Brown |
| Green | Cream | Cream/ Green | Cream/Grey | Black |
| Wine | Cream | Wine/ Cream | Old Rose | Black |
| Blue | Pale Blue | Blue/ Grey | Dark Blue | Black |

Colour in morning dress is fun – for the rich anyway, but if you are considering buying an expensive suit specially made, it is probably better to opt for traditional colours. The current relaxation of many established rules of etiquette and the trend of finding one's own style, bought in a mood of colourful and sophisticated abandon, may not last as long as your morning suit.

Owing to the expense involved and the fact that buying a morning suit is only economical if you are going to attend formal occasions on a regular basis, it is more usual these days, to hire morning dress.

## Hiring a Morning Suit

For the majority of best men, a hired suit is often appropriate enough. There are many reputable establishments who can supply both the traditional black coat and pin stripes or the plain grey morning suit.

You should bear in mind that the summer months are very popular for weddings and for a number of other social functions such as Ascot. It is wise to reserve your wedding suit well in advance of the wedding date and of course you must get it back within the time specified otherwise you will find yourself paying additional charges.

The bride may have strong views about what the men should wear. She may have a particular colour scheme in mind for herself, her attendants and the church flowers. For example, her own dress may be white with a pink sash, her bridesmaids and page boys may be dressed in sweet pea colours of blue, pink and lilac to echo the flowers in her bouquet, church decorations and reception flowers. It could work well if the groom, best man and ushers wore lilac silk cravats with pale grey morning suits.

## · THE WEDDING SUIT ·

For a less formal wedding, the principal men may choose lounge suits with matching accessories. These are very popular and may be worn again after the wedding. As is the case with formal attire, it is important to check on the bride's choice of colour scheme so that overall continuity is achieved. The colours of suits and accessories should match the rest of the wedding party. If the bridesmaids are wearing peach, for example, it will look best if the

31

men's shirts, ties and handkerchiefs and so on are in a complementary colour.

As any woman will tell you, a wedding is always a good excuse for a new outfit and there is no reason why this should not also apply to men. As best man take care that you do not outshine the groom. A simply cut two- or three-piece lounge suit is perhaps the best buy of all because it automatically becomes part of your everyday wardrobe after the great event. It is well worth looking around some of the big department stores for off-the-peg styles. Lightweight suits, well cut and in conservative colours, are a good buy for those who are stock sizes and will cost far less than a tailor-made garment.

Whatever you wear, one rule is always the same: shoes must be polished to a mirror-shine (and you should remind the groom to remove the price tag from new shoes!).

## · CLOTHES FOR A SECOND · WEDDING

For a second wedding, there is no reason to suggest that the groom and best man should not wear formal attire or if they prefer, something less formal. However, though the church ceremony is exactly the same where a bride happens to be a widow, tradition calls for less formality and suggests dark lounge suits rather than the formal attire usual at a bride's first wedding.

# · CLOTHES FOR A CIVIL WEDDING ·

There are no rules about the right and wrong clothes to wear at the registry office. Most registrars will see jeans, tee-shirts, blazers, sports jackets, lounge suits and even morning suits all pass before their bewildered eyes during the course of one day's work.

Your choice of clothes will depend on the views of the bride and groom. Take your cue from them, imitate their style but do not outshine them.

One point which many people forget is that the traditional white wedding dress with full train and veil were designed to create an impact inside the church where the aisle can show the garment off to its full advantage. Very formal attire like this is not really practical for the often cramped conditions at most registry offices and you will find that, in the same way, a morning suit will dominate rather than complement the surroundings.

# · THE BUTTONHOLES ·

White carnations used to be the traditional buttonhole for the principal men at weddings and are still popular. However, today wedding parties are more adventurous in their choice and the groom may wear a different colour to the other principal men. Alternatives to the white carnation are the clove (red) carnation, the garnet rose, the cornflower, the orchid or the camelia, although the latter is sometimes rather fragile. The groom, best man and fathers sometimes have double red carnations and some choose white, pink or yellow roses and ushers usually have single red or white buttonholes.

Convention holds that the groom should pay for his own buttonhole and for those of the best man and the ushers. These should be ordered at least three weeks before the wedding from a local florist and collected before the ceremony and taken to the bride's parents' home. If the wedding is to take place on unfamiliar ground, the bride could order the buttonholes together with all the other wedding flowers and arrange for them to be delivered to the reception premises, in which case the best man will need to collect them from here when he visits to leave the groom's going-away clothes and before collecting the groom.

## · HAIR ·

The smartest suit will be spoilt if your hair is not well cut and groomed. Arrange for a haircut about three weeks before the wedding, or a week before if you are sure that there will be no disaster with the scissors!

## · DRESSING ·

Though the best man is supposed to help the groom to dress for his wedding, this is unnecessary with today's modern clothes. In previous days with the magnificent velvets, silks, satins, socks, stockings and shoe buckles worn by the groom, the best man needed the services of a valet to help him dress the nervous groom! Today, the best man usually arrives at the groom's house as he is dressing.

## · **DRESS REHEARSAL** ·

A quick dress rehearsal for the groom and best man a week or so before the wedding will provide a final check that nothing is forgotten. New shirts should be unpacked and ironed, price tags removed from the soles of new shoes and everything should feel and look good together.

# · 4 ·
# *Parties*

## · ENGAGEMENT ·

Many couples celebrate their engagement with a
party to which they will, most probably, invite their
prospective best man.

## · CEREMONY REHEARSAL ·

Some couples hold a party after the ceremony
rehearsal as it is an enjoyable way to share some time
with the principal people during a very busy period
and to exchange wedding gifts. The rehearsal party is
normally the responsibility of the groom's family.

## · THE STAG PARTY ·

After the planning is over and before the action
begins, some couples like to celebrate separately
with friends of their own sex. On these occasions
friends play the devil and the groom particularly
risks being the butt of some pretty adolescent
pranks. In primitive terms, these parties represent
the shaking out of the evil spirits that could yet
hamper the couple's marriage. The rule that only
unmarried men were invited to the stag night is
often ignored today, but it is still usually an event

for relatives and friends of around the groom's own age. The bride and her friends have their own celebrations – the hen party.

It is the groom's decision as to how he would prefer to spend the evening but it is traditionally the best man's responsibility to organise the celebration and should be one of his least arduous duties. The groom may prefer to handle the organising himself but normally the groom informs the best man of the friends whom he would like invited and the best man does the rest. Although the evening can include anything from a full-scale party with entertainment laid on, the emphasis is usually on informality, so written invitations are unnecessary. The date, time and location of the party are usually spread by word of mouth.

The majority of stag parties are very informal, usually held in the local pub and followed by an inexpensive meal. Chinese and Indian restaurants seem to rank high as a final port of call for a bachelor night out, possibly because they are more willing to welcome late night eaters than many others. If speeches are included, two are sufficient and these should take place at the coffee stage of a meal or about half way through a drinks party. The stag party is a good opportunity for you to test your speech-making powers. Everyone will have made some cracks about the groom's last bachelor minutes ebbing away and there is no reason why you should not add your own comments. The best man will aim for plenty of laughs at the groom's expense and the groom will reply. You should add your congratulations too: assure the groom he has done the right thing and wish him all the luck in the world.

It is wise to book a table in advance if you are planning to eat at a restaurant after the pub outing especially if there will be a large group, so that there are no last-minute disappointments and all the party can be seated together.

Although the best man should be allowed to enjoy the evening, he must remember his responsibility for ensuring that the groom returns home safely. On no account should anyone be allowed to drive if they have had a drink! Transport arrangements need to be made before the event and the best man should ensure that all attenders have made suitable arrangements. To economise, or to be sure, the party-goers could always walk if the venue is local. It is a very good idea to walk to the pub and/or restaurant if they are in your vicinity, or at least take a taxi. Whatever you decide, it is essential that the groom is not allowed to drive.

Traditionally the stag party takes place on the eve of the wedding – but this can be disastrous and the bride should dissuade the groom and best man from arranging the party so close to the wedding date. Try if possible to persuade the groom to hold the party a week before the event to give everyone a good chance to recover from the predictable results of over-indulgence in sentimental alcohol.

The guests will normally include the ushers, close friends of the groom, brothers of the bride and groom and sometimes the fathers of the bride and groom, but, even if the fathers are determined adolescents, the generation gap can put a blight on the proceedings.

At one time the stag party was a very formal affair and the guests wore black tie and dinner jackets for the occasion, but this was in an era when men's drinking clubs were a good deal more popular than they are today.

Traditionally, the groom should pay for the entire evening's entertainment but nowadays, drinks for an entire evening, plus the cost of a meal for twenty or so voracious men, could be astronomical. Unless the groom can afford it, you should explain that the meal is optional and at guests' own expense. The best man should let all attenders know what they will be expected to pay in advance so that everyone is spared embarrassment on the night itself.

On the stag night you should collect the groom from his home and escort him to the pub and offer to take charge of the kitty. You should know what sort of drinks your friends like, spirits or beer, so make sure that the groom has enough cash. You could take along some spare cash of your own – the groom can always pay you back if funds run short.

It has been known for a best man to take his duties seriously enough to exist on a half pint of beer for the whole evening, but, providing you do not intend to drive why not enjoy the occasion! Everyone else will.

Your last duty of the night is to see the groom to his front door safely. Do not leave until you are quite sure that he is inside.

## · POST-WEDDING PARTY ·

It is traditional for the newly-weds to entertain both sets of parents, then the best man together with the maid/matron of honour, bridesmaids and any other attendants in their new home after the wedding when the festivities have subsided and they are more settled.

# · 5 ·
# *The Week Before the Wedding*

## · THE GO-BETWEEN ·

The relay system established earlier in the wedding preparations between yourself and the bride, groom and ushers will now be vitally important: any snags at this stage could affect procedures on the wedding day. The best idea is to refer to a list of things to do (the checklist below and those at the end of the book should prove useful for this purpose) and tick off each item one by one when each query has been dealt with to the satisfaction of everyone concerned. The following list should give you some idea of the points you should have in mind.

1   Has the groom bought the wedding ring and does he have it safe?
2   Has everyone who needs one ordered his wedding suit:
   a)  Groom?
   b)  Ushers?
   c)  Yourself?
   Make sure that none of the principal men is planning to leave the collection of a morning suit until the morning of the wedding!
3   Flowers
   a)  If the groom is ordering buttonholes from a

local florist, does the florist know where to deliver the goods (the groom's home)?

b) If you are collecting the buttonholes on behalf of the groom, have you contacted the florist to check that the flowers will be ready when you call?

c) If the bride is arranging all the flowers including the buttonholes, has she arranged to have them all delivered elsewhere?

4 Transport

a) Have you made a list of taxi firms in your area, in case the car breaks down on the way to the church?

b) If neither you or the groom will be using a car on the day of the wedding:

i) Is a taxi ordered to take you and the groom to the church?

ii) Do you have transport from the church to the reception?

iii) Do all the guests have adequate transport?

c) If the bride and groom are not planning to use their own car or someone else's for their honeymoon:

i) Have you ordered a car to take them to the station/airport/new home?

5 Are the groom's documents in order and does he have them safe?

a) Passport;

b) Driving licence;

c) Traveller's cheques/foreign currency if honeymooning abroad.

d) Has he remembered all the necessary inoculations?

e) Has he remembered to collect the banns

certificate from his local minister (if he lives outside the parish where he is to be married)?

f) Does he have all the necessary insurances, travel tickets, etc. for travelling on the continent by car?

6 Do you know how much the wedding fees will be? Although the groom is responsible for the cost of the fees to the minister, organist, choir, bell-ringers, you will be handing over the money. There may be additional tips to the verger, but generally the minister will charge one comprehensive price and pay the people concerned himself.

7 Do you have enough spare cash for the wedding day?

8 Does the groom have enough money ready for both the wedding day and his honeymoon?

9 Have you checked on the layout of the church, i.e. the location of the vestry?

10 Does the minister have strong views about:

a) The time you are expected to arrive at the ceremony – naturally you will be expected to be early, but sometimes the minister will ask to meet you and the groom in the vestry twenty minutes before the ceremony begins to pay the fees before rather than after the wedding.

b) Confetti: most ministers have strict views about paper confetti. Detail an usher to mention this as people enter the church.

c) Photographs: The minister may forbid the taking of photographs inside the church. The official photographer may be permitted to take shots of the couple signing the register in the vestry and perhaps one as they walk back along the aisle after the ceremony. You can be sure that all ministers will object to a host of light bulbs popping throughout the ceremony! Ushers should warn people with cameras as they arrive at the church. Nothing could be more embarrassing than the vicar calling a halt to the proceedings to admonish amateur photographers!

11 Does the groom have all the necessary clothes for his honeymoon?

12 Have you collected the order of service sheets from the bride's home?

13 Has the bride remembered that her going-away clothes must be left at the reception premises before the wedding, together with her honeymoon luggage? Check with the maid/matron of honour (or chief bridesmaid).

14 Are the reception staff aware that you are coming to deposit the groom's luggage and going-away clothes before the wedding ceremony?

15 Do you know what time you are all expected to leave the premises?

16 Do the ushers know what each should be doing on the wedding day?

17 Is there anything you can do to help the bride's family such as:
   a) Transporting the cake
   b) Collecting flowers for the church or reception
   c) Helping with the marquee (if the reception is to be held in a garden)?

18 Is everyone agreed on the sequence of events at the reception?

19 Has the groom remembered to remove the price tag from the bottom of his shoes (if they are new)?

20 Have you remembered the bride and groom's wedding present?

21 Have you reminded the bride's family that any telegrams delivered to their home on the morning of the wedding must be brought along to the reception?

22 Is the couple's new house insured against theft? Nothing could be worse than all the wedding gifts being stolen while the couple are away. You or someone from the bride's family could perhaps check on the premises while the couple are honeymooning.

23 Do you have an umbrella, just in case?

24 Are you keeping the groom calm?

## · THE WEDDING REHEARSAL ·

Sometimes a minister will specially request an informal rehearsal for all the principal people involved in the wedding ceremony. This is usually necessary only when the wedding is to be a very large, formal affair, with numerous attendants. However, the bridal party may feel happier if they are sure of what is expected of them. Most people find it a useful way of sorting out any last-minute worries concerning procedure. It is a splendid opportunity to be introduced to the vicar and to ask any questions which are bothering you.

The rehearsal is held inside the church up to a week before the wedding so that procedures remain fresh in the minds of the wedding party members. The minister will probably run through the ceremony and point out where each person should be during the service. The bride, groom, best man, bridesmaids and the bride's father need to attend. The bride's mother and the groom's parents may also wish to attend.

Some couples hold a get-together for the principal people after the rehearsal to thank them for their support. This would be a suitable time for wedding party members to present the couple with wedding gifts, so that they may be unwrapped at leisure, and likewise for the couple to present their gifts to the attendants. Use the rehearsal get-together as a chance to check on the arrangements, to get to know the close members of both families and finalise arrangements. Going through everything in detail at the rehearsal will be time well spent and may save frantic moments later on.

## · WEDDING GIFT FROM THE · BEST MAN

After the wedding rehearsal is perhaps the best time to pass on your wedding gift to the bride and groom.

Some more unusual gift ideas might include:
    Tickets to events
    Season tickets to sports, musical or theatrical
      events
    Gift vouchers
    Games
    Holiday equipment
    Leisure equipment
    Hobby items
    A regular supply of specialities such as wines,
      fruit or flowers delivered at specified intervals.

## · GIFT FOR THE BEST MAN ·

Gifts from the bride and groom to members of the wedding party show appreciation for their participation and contribution to the wedding. It is customary for the couple to pass on their gifts to the wedding party either at the rehearsal get-together or on the morning of the wedding.

## · OUTWITTING THE WEATHER ·

In the temperate but highly erratic climate of Britain, the weather will often catch people unawares at a wedding. You and the ushers at least can be prepared for the worst by taking a couple of large black umbrellas along to the wedding with you. If the weather looks uncompromisingly fine, you can always leave them in the car.

# ·2·
# The Day

# ·6·
# Getting to the Church on Time

When it actually comes to the day of the wedding you will probably need little advice on ways to make yourself wake up in good time. However, if this is not one of your strong points, arrange an early morning wake-up call. Once you are up and about, ring the groom to see that he is not snoring away his last bachelor minutes.

Opinions are divided about the need to ring the bride's home to see if her parents need any help. On one hand you may be roped in for an unforeseen trip to collect four dozen sausage rolls forgotten by the caterer, on the other hand you want to be regarded as the world's best best man, so it is probably safer to check that everything is fine at their end and avoid last-minute panics later in the day.

The time that you actually arrive at the groom's house to escort him to the church will depend on the length of the journey, and you should by now have checked all this out.

If you have offered to collect buttonholes on behalf of the groom, do this before you arrive at his home as leaving this until later may cause delay. Similarly, the groom's going-away clothes and honeymoon cases may be taken to the reception venue early rather than making a detour on route to the church.

If the reception is to be held a long distance from the church and it has not been possible to visit earlier in the day and you are using a private car to get the groom to the church, the groom's belongings may be left in the car carefully arranged over the seat. If the groom is to use his car for the honeymoon, arrange to leave it at the reception premises the day before the ceremony, otherwise someone else will have to drive it from the church to the reception.

If the wedding is to be held at a local church, arrive at the groom's home about an hour and a half before the service is due to begin.

Traditionally one of your duties is to help the groom to dress, but unless his nerves are really shot to pieces, he should be able to perform this function quite adequately. You will, however, need to check over all his documents to ensure that they are in order and that they are all there – two minds on the subject are invariably better than one – but under conditions of stress, i.e. your speech and his nerves, it is better to check off a previously prepared checklist. (The checklist at the back of the book should prove useful.)

You should arrive at the church about half an hour before the ceremony is due to start.

Buttonholes should be secured and the ushers should have the order of service sheets ready. The best man and groom may be required to see the minister and pay the fees before the ceremony (unless arranged otherwise). It is advisable to pay church fees at this point rather than immediately after the ceremony. You will then be able to join the recessional and oversee transport arrangements. Since the minister puts in so much effort, the groom might consider making a special personal donation to the church.

There are usually a few minutes to spare while the official photographer takes the obligatory photograph of the groom and best man shaking hands in the church porch and then everyone takes their places for the arrival of the guests and finally the bride herself.

The ushers line up on the left side of the church entrance, greet the congregation and hand out hymn books, prayer books and/or order of service sheets. They advise the congregation of any restrictions regarding photography and/or confetti throwing. Tossing paper confetti at the bride and groom is a relatively new idea and since it can make such a mess of the churchyard and is often not allowed for this reason, modern practice is to revert to the tossing of rice, grain, fresh flowers, rose petals, or confetti of the type which birds will eat such as wild bird food. It is wise to discourage guests from using the 'litter' type. If the throwing of confetti is allowed, there may be a charge. Local litter laws should be checked beforehand and observed at all times; if the church door opens directly onto the street, paper confetti will not be allowed.

The ushers conduct people to pews escorting any unescorted lady to her seat; the bride's family and friends on the left and the groom's family and friends on the right.

If there are cases of death or divorce in the family, the situation must be handled tactfully and with the understanding to suit the circumstances. If either set of parents is divorced and remarried, the mother sits in the first pew (as she would do normally) with her new partner, and the father and his new partner take the second pew on the relevant side of the church. In cases of such sensitivity, the ushers must be made aware of circumstances in advance.

Wedding ceremonies cannot really be private in that no one can be prevented from attending. Thus, well-wishers and friends do not need to be invited to the ceremony so there may be more congregation than expected!

# GETTING TO THE CHURCH ON TIME

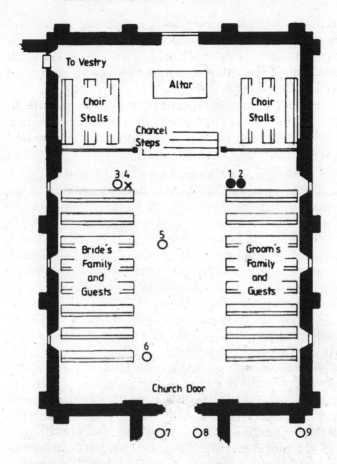

## Church Seating

1  Groom
2. Best Man
3  Bride's Mother
4. Seat for Bride's Father
5. and 6.  Usher (Guests to their seats)

7.  Usher (to give out hymn sheets)
8.  Usher (Escort for Bride's Mother)
9.  Usher (To direct Guests to Car Parks)

# ·7·

# The Ceremony

The bride's mother should be one of the last people to arrive at the church. She usually travels to the church with the bridesmaids, who remain in the church porch to wait for the arrival of the bride. The chief usher should escort the bride's mother to her seat in the front pew on the left of the chancel steps facing the altar. The bride's mother should leave room for her husband to take his place when he has given away his daughter.

As soon as the bride arrives, the ushers should move quietly to their seats at the rear of the church before the procession begins.

The full choral service in the Church of England takes about thirty minutes from start to finish. The minister will meet the bride in the church porch and the procession will begin with the chief chorister leading the way with the standard Cross. Behind him range the choir, the minister, the bride on her father's right arm and then the attendants.

The organist will be watching to see that everyone is ready and when they are he will play the entrance music selected by the bride. This is usually a slow march or a reasonably gentle piece of music. As the first chords are played the congregation will rise to their feet and at this moment the best man and groom move from their

# THE CEREMONY

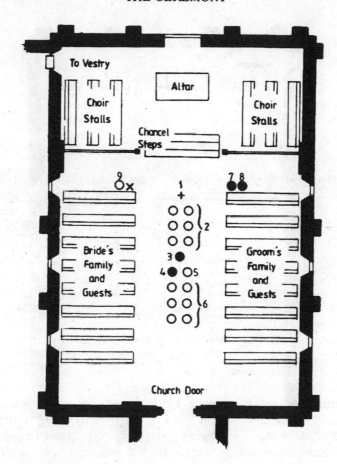

## Procession

1. Chief Chorister
2. Choir
3. Minister
4. Bride's Father
5. Bride
6. Attendants
7. Groom
8. Best Man
9. Bride's Mother
x. Space for Bride's Father

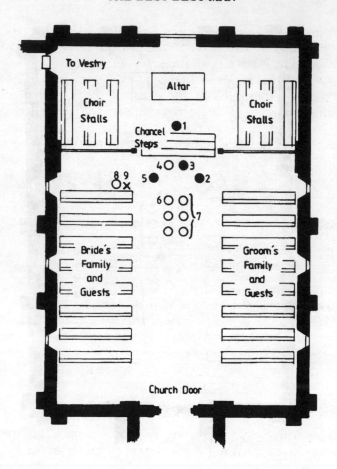

## *At the Chancel Steps*

1  Minister
2. Best Man
3  Groom
4. Bride
5. Bride's Father

6. Chief Bridesmaid
7. Attendants
8. Bride's Mother
9. Space for Bride's Father

seats to the chancel steps, standing a little to the right so that the choir and minister have room to walk through to the chancel.

When the choir has taken its place and the bridal party is assembled at the chancel steps, the chief bridesmaid steps forward to lift the bride's veil and take the bride's bouquet so that both her hands are free when the time comes to put on the ring. Where there are no bridesmaids, the bride can pass her bouquet to her father who can turn and hand it to the bride's mother, if the front pew is near enough to the chancel steps. In a large church the pews may be some feet away from the bridal party. In this case ask the minister beforehand if a pew hassock could be strategically placed near the bridal party for the bouquet to rest on until the bride's father can hand it over to the bride's mother when his part in the ceremony is over.

If the aisle is very narrow, the bride's father and the best man should stand slightly behind the bridal couple, moving forward only when it is time for them to play their part in the ceremony.

## · THE ORDER OF SERVICE ·

This will vary according to the wishes of the minister performing the ceremony, or those of the couple concerned. Some ministers often prefer to conduct the marriage before any hymns are sung and the address may be made from the altar or from the chancel steps.

# THE BEST BEST MAN

Shown below is a typical order of service:

ENTRANCE (PROCESSIONAL) MUSIC
HYMN
THE MARRIAGE
THE PSALM
PRAYERS (at the altar)
THE ADDRESS
HYMN
THE BLESSING
SIGNING OF THE REGISTER (choir or organ music)
EXIT (RECESSIONAL) MUSIC

After the first hymn the minister will begin the marriage ceremony. The minister will explain the significance of marriage and the reasons why it was originally ordained. He then calls on the congregation to declare any impediment to the marriage. The bride and groom are asked if they know of any lawful impediment to their marriage.

The minister then asks each of the couple in turn whether they are prepared to accept the other in marriage, according to the laws of the Church:

"Wilt thou have this woman to thy wedded wife?" And to the bride:

"Wilt thou have this man to thy wedded husband?"

Both should answer "I will".

The minister will then ask:

"Who giveth this woman to be married to this man?"

The bride's father will say nothing, but he will pass his daughter's right hand to the minister.

The groom will take her hand in his right hand.

Repeating the words after the minister, the groom

will make his vow first:

"I ..., take thee ..., to my wedded wife ...".

They release their hands and the bride will take the groom's right hand in her own.

Repeating the words after the minister the bride will make her vow:

"I ..., take thee ..., to my wedded husband ...".

When the vows have been completed the minister will offer the best man the open face of the prayer book, onto which he should place the ring(s). The groom will take the ring and place it on the third finger of the bride's left hand with the words:

"With this ring, I thee wed ..."

At this point in the ceremony the bride's father and the best man should return to their seats at the front of the church while the rest of the service continues. The minister will wait until they have taken their places before he asks the bride and groom to kneel and the rest of the congregation to pray. A blessing follows the prayers and then the minister will lead the bride and groom to the altar while the congregation sings the psalm.

The prayers that follow may be said or intoned, whichever the bride and groom prefer, or the minister will follow the usual custom of the church.

The address usually follows the prayers, and the final hymn will conclude the service.

## · SIGNING THE REGISTER ·

The minister will then lead the bride and groom into the vestry. The congregation will sit and listen to the choir or the organist while the register is being signed. As soon as the bride and groom move into the vestry, the rest of the bridal party will follow. This will include both sets of parents, the attendants, who should all move off in a line, and yourself. Make sure that the chief bridesmaid has remembered the bride's bouquet – if you should see it lying in the front pew, carry it through to the vestry yourself, as the bride will need it for her exit from the church.

In the vestry there is a round of congratulations, kisses and handshaking and then the bride and groom will sign the register. The bride signs first in her single name. When the couple have both signed, the minister will ask for two witnesses, who must be over the age of eighteen. The best man and the chief bridesmaid may be requested to do this, but sometimes the minister will ask the fathers of the bride and groom to sign, because their names appear automatically on the marriage certificate and there will be no problems in deciphering the signatures should it ever be necessary.

One or two photographs may be taken while the register is being signed and then the bride and groom will lead the recession (that is, the procession back along the aisle) out of the church. The organist will strike up the recessional music which is invariably a triumphal march and the bell-ringers, hearing the notes of the organ, will chime forth the glad tiding to all and sundry.

Her bouquet restored to her, the bride walks on her husband's left side, leaving his sword arm free to defend her (this probably applied quite often in times gone by!). The bride and groom lead the recession, followed by the attendants who pair off, each usher escorting a bridesmaid along the aisle. Next are the parents of the bride and groom followed by the maid/matron of honour (or chief bridesmaid) with the best man. However, it is acceptable for the wedding party to leave as they entered – bridesmaids together with ushers together if preferred. If the minister has asked that all the fees should be paid after the ceremony, the best man will stay behind in the vestry to settle the accounts, while the recession is in progress.

## · THE PHOTOGRAPHS ·

Official photographs usually take about twenty minutes to complete and you, as best man, will appear in several of these. With the advancement of technological achievements and creative editing, professional videographers can now produce tapes of exceptional quality and many brides choose to have their wedding videoed in addition to or instead of the traditional photographs. Most couples will want at least one large group photograph of all the close relatives and it is the organisation of just such a shot which will take the time. Your voice of sanity can help the photographer to arrange all the smaller people in the front row and make sure that those behind are looking over the shoulders of the row in front and not over the top of their heads! When a professional photographer is employed, guests should be tactfully instructed not to take their own photographs when the expert is working.

Rainy weddings are unfortunate and nearly always catch people unawares, but the excited bride and groom are less likely to notice the weather than the guests who may not be able to take refuge in the church porch because there is another wedding going on inside. In this case it is

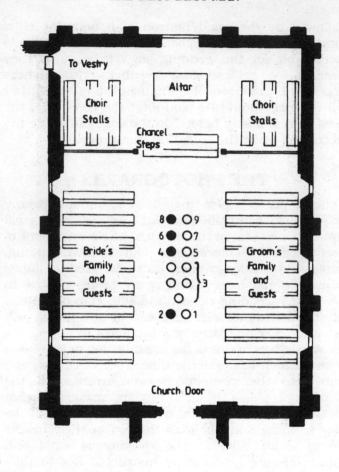

*Recession with the best man*

1  Bride
2. Groom
3  Attendants
4. Groom's Father
5. Bride's Mother

6. Bride's Father
7. Groom's Mother
8. Best Man
9. Chief Bridesmaid

# THE CEREMONY

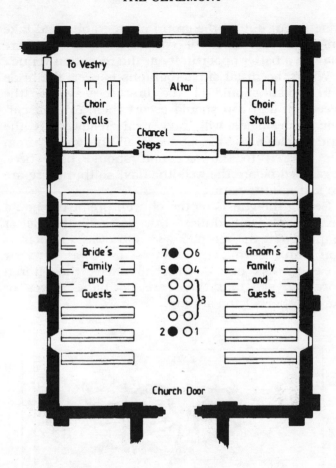

*Recession without the best man*

1  Bride
2. Groom
3  Attendants (including Chief Bridesmaid)
4. Bride's Mother
5. Groom's Father
6. Groom's Mother
7. Bride's Father

wise to cut out all the group photographs and take only one or two of the couple themselves. There may be a better opportunity at the reception venue.

When the ritual of photographs is over, the bride and groom should be the first to leave for the reception and you should escort them to their car. The bridesmaids will leave next, followed by the bride's parents. Transport for all the guests from the church to the reception should have been organised before the wedding day, so that there are no last-minute panics.

Seeing the guests off the church premises should be one of your duties, but you will be better employed at the reception, so slip away as soon as you can, leaving the ushers to cope in your absence. Ask one of them to check the church porch to see that there are no hats, gloves or service sheets lying around.

# ·8·
# *Other Weddings and Circumstances*

## · SECOND WEDDINGS ·

There has been a certain amount of relaxation in the views of some ministers about remarrying a divorced person in the established Church, but it is still a rare occurrence. Most ministers still hold the very rigid belief that in the eyes of God a marriage is valid until death and whatever the circumstances, while both participants are still alive, another marriage is not possible let alone permissible.

Remarriage of widowed people is of course, quite acceptable, but the minister must be consulted for his views on a number of points. In the first place he may feel that the bride should not wear a veil, although he is unlikely these days to object to her wearing white. He may object to the presence of attendants and may feel that the choice of certain hymns and music are not appropriate for a second wedding; he may object to the pealing of bells.

In most cases, however, the ceremony and organization will be exactly the same as for a first wedding in church and the duties of the best man will also be the same, except that his speech will need to be more serious in tone.

## · SERVICE OF BLESSING ·

For the couple who have not been able to marry in church, perhaps because of different religious convictions, or because one or both has been divorced, a service of blessing may be arranged.

This is a brief and very simple service to bless a marriage and can take place at any time after a civil ceremony. A service of blessing is not, and must not pretend to be, a marriage ceremony. There are no vows, no hymns, no bells or any of the conventional formalities of a wedding ceremony.

The bride and groom, together with a few family members or friends, will meet in the church as for a normal service. The minister conducting the service will give a brief address, followed by prayers to bless the marriage and there is sometimes a gospel reading. The question of dress, the presence of flowers and music should be discussed with the minister. There are no duties for the best man to perform at the service, but if a reception follows the blessing, he will be required to help with its organisation and to make a speech.

## · DOUBLE WEDDINGS ·

Since most brides would be extremely reluctant to share the limelight on their wedding day it is usually only twins or sisters in the same age group who share the same friends, who would welcome a double wedding.

The procedures are the same as for a wedding for one couple in that there will be a best man for each groom and attendants for the brides. Meetings and discussions will take place between six rather than three people (two brides, two grooms and two best men). One important point which must be established early on is what everyone should wear. If there are to be nearly a dozen people at the front of the church there should be a certain sense of uniformity in their dress – try to imagine how it will look from where the congregation is sitting.

If it is possible for the couples concerned to be married in a church with two central aisles, seating arrangements for the ceremony will be quite simple but the layout of most churches is not quite so convenient. When there is only one aisle the families of the two grooms will have to share the favoured positions at the front of the church on the right, and there may only be a need for one set of ushers.

At the start of the ceremony the two grooms, each with his own best man, will take their places at the head of the aisle, the future husband of the first and eldest bride will stand slightly to the right of the chancel steps to allow the choir and minister to walk past and the second groom and his best man will stand on the right of the first pair.

When the brides make their entrance, the eldest will be escorted by her father, the younger bride may be escorted by a brother or another male member of her family. When the brides are not sisters, the bride of the eldest bridegroom will enter first. When the procession reaches the chancel steps the first bride will stand next to her groom, on his left; the second bride will take her place to the right of the first couple and her escort can immediately return to his seat.

The ceremony is usually divided into sections with each couple making their vows in turn. The father can give both brides away before returning to his seat. If the brides are not sisters, the second bride's father will stand between the first couple's best man and his own daughter.

It is most common for the brides to share the same attendants, although each should have her own chief bridesmaid to take the flowers while the ceremony is in progress.

The recession is led by the eldest bride and her husband, followed immediately by the second couple. Since the bride's parents can only appear once in the procession, the parents of the second groom may have to walk down the aisle together, or escort and be escorted by one chief bridesmaid and one best man. The procession, recession, escorts and order for speeches at the reception will need thorough rehearsal so that there is no confusion on the day.

## · ROMAN CATHOLIC WEDDINGS ·

The religious ceremony in the Roman Catholic Church must be accompanied by a civil declaration to legalise the marriage. In the established Church most ministers are authorised to perform the registration of the marriage, but in the Roman Catholic Church registration should be carried out by a state official.

There are two types of Roman Catholic wedding: a simple ceremony and a full Nuptial Mass. The church calendar forbids a Nuptial Mass to take place during Lent and between the first Sunday of Advent and December 26th. A Nuptial Mass cannot be celebrated unless both the bride and groom are Catholics.

The procession, church seating and the exchange of vows at the Catholic wedding are very similar to

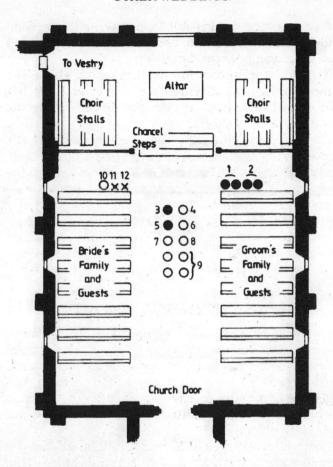

## The Double Wedding procession

1  Groom and Best Man (A)
2.  Groom and Best Man (B)
3  Brides' Father
4.  Bride (A)
5.  Escort for Bride (B)
6.  Bride (B)
7.  Chief Bridesmaid (A)
8.  Chief Bridesmaid (B)
9.  Attendants
10.  Mother of both Brides
11.  Seat for Brides' Father
12.  Seat for Escort (B)

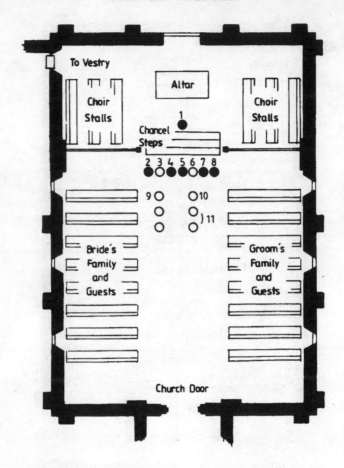

*The Double Wedding at the chancel steps*

1   Minister
2.  Father of both Brides
3   Bride (A)
4.  Groom (A)
5.  Best Man (A)
6.  Bride (B)

7.  Groom (B)
8.  Best Man (B)
9.  Chief Bridesmaid (A)
10. Chief Bridesmaid (B)
11. Attendants

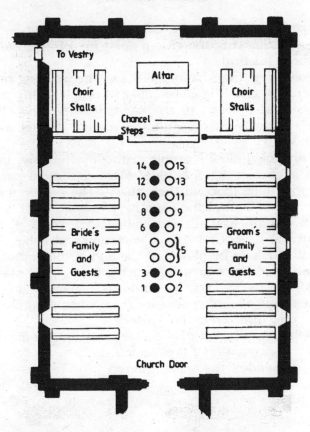

## The Recession at the Double Wedding

1  Groom (A)
2. Bride (A)
3  Groom (B)
4. Bride (B)
5. Attendants
6. Brides' Father (B)
7. Mother of Groom (A)
8. Father of Groom (A)

9. Brides' Mother
10. Groom (B) Father
11. Groom (B) Mother
12. Best Man (A)
13. Chief Bridesmaid (A)
14. Best Man (B)
15. Chief Bridesmaid (B)

those of the established Church, but in addition to the wedding ring the groom must present gold and silver to his bride.

Following the exchange of vows, the wedding ring ceremony and the blessing, the couple, with two witnesses, proceed to the sacristy where the civil declaration is made, and the register signed and witnessed.

This concludes a simple Catholic ceremony, but in the case of a full Nuptial Mass the bridal party returns once more to the church. The couple take their place behind the sanctuary rails and the best man, parents and attendants take their seats at the front of the church. It is sometimes possible for small stools to be placed at the end of the pews for small attendants to sit on during the Nuptial Mass but if this is not possible the ushers must remember to leave spaces for them when the guests are being directed to their places.

Holy Communion may be taken by any members of the congregation if they so wish.

At the end of the Mass, the recession begins with the bride and groom leading the way and the attendants moving into their places from the pews.

## · NONCONFORMIST WEDDINGS ·

These are much more simple in style than those of either the Anglican or Roman Churches, although the wording of the ceremony is almost identical. The best man's duties are the same, however, although if he has never attended a nonconformist wedding he should ask the bride exactly what form the service will take and ask her to explain any minor differences in wording or the order of service.

## · JEWISH WEDDINGS ·

It is extremely unlikely that a best man at a Jewish wedding will not himself be a member of the faith, but, if you should find yourself doing the honours, you must inform yourself about all the details of the ceremony, which will differ considerably from those of the Christian Churches.

The wedding ceremony in a synagogue takes place under a canopy, which is often beautifully decorated with flowers. The groom is escorted to his place by male members of his family and the same escorts will return to the synagogue door to collect the bride and deliver her to the groom's right hand. Without exception the congregation must have their heads covered; the men and women sit on opposite sides of the synagogue.

The details of the ceremony will vary according to the rites of the Orthodox or Reformed Synagogue. The Orthodox service will include the Seven Benedictions, which are chanted by the rabbi, and the groom will break a wine glass beneath his heel to symbolise the destruction of the Temple in Jerusalem.

Although a separate civil contract is made, it is still necessary to sign the marriage register at the synagogue and to add the names of two witnesses.

## · CIVIL WEDDINGS ·

A registry office wedding is a simpler and much less formal affair than a church wedding lasting only about ten minutes. It entails no religious service and all that is required is that the marriage vows are exchanged before a superintendent registrar and the register signed with two witnesses being present who also sign the register.

Those who choose to marry in a registry office may be divorced and unable to remarry in church, they may hold different religious beliefs, or religious convictions may have no meaning for them.

The brief nature of the ceremony does not lend itself to the usual formalities undertaken by the best man at a church wedding ceremony. However, there is no reason why the bride and groom should not be attended by a full wedding party if this is their wish and if facilities allow but, often, a registry office cannot accommodate too many people so the guests are likely to be rather limited. Seating or standing arrangements in the registry office are very informal. Flower arrangements are provided and everything is done to make the ceremony as special as possible. The wedding party may dress informally or traditionally. The best man can hand over the ring(s) to the groom at the appropriate moment in the ceremony, but strictly speaking there is no need for a ring to play any part in the proceedings as this has no legal significance under civil law – although, most brides will keep this tradition even if they are willing to dispense with most of the others.

The bride and groom will arrive at the registry office together, and, in the presence of at least two witnesses, apart from the officiating registrar, they will declare that there is no lawful impediment to their marriage. Each repeats: "I do solemnly declare that I know not of any lawful impediment why I [name] may not be joined in matrimony to [name]". The couple are advised of the solemn and binding nature of the marriage. They will then call upon the attendant audience to witness their marriage and vows are exchanged: "I call upon these persons here present to witness that I [name] do take [name] to be my lawful wedded husband/wife". The ring is placed on the bride's third finger. The register is signed by two witnesses (usually the bride's father and the best man but they can be complete strangers) after the bride and groom have signed, and the registrar and superintendent registrar will also add their signatures.

A registry office ceremony may take place between sunrise and 6 pm. It is worth noting that most registry offices are closed on Sundays and from noon on a Saturday and are booked well in advance on such popular days.

The best man should certainly make himself available to get the couple to the registry office on time. Civil weddings run to a strict timetable and if the couple are late they often have to wait until later in the day, or miss their turn altogether. The order in which family and friends enter and leave the registry office is unimportant but the bride and groom should be allowed to travel to the reception alone.

Normal procedures for a reception can follow the civil wedding, although formal invitations sent out to guests other than immediate family, should request their company at the reception only. Rules for the formality or informality of reception following a registry office wedding are the same as those following a church wedding.

Although traditionally held in a registry office, civil ceremonies can now take place in other premises, as long as the place is licensed for this purpose. Such places may include hotels and historic buildings.

# ·9·
# *The Reception*

First to arrive at the reception premises will be the bride and groom, followed by the attendants and parents. If you have assigned the task of ensuring transport from the church to the reception to the chief usher, you should also be among the first to arrive at the reception venue so that you can speak to the toastmaster about the sequence of events and provide the names of the speakers. Ask the two sets of parents for any telegrams and messages which may have arrived at their homes before they left for the wedding and check for any that may have arrived at the reception venue.

The chief bridesmaid should take charge of the bride's bouquet and ensure that it remains in a cool place while the reception is in progress.

## · THE RECEIVING LINE ·

There can never be hard and fast rules about this because the situation will vary from wedding to wedding. Most receptions have a receiving line and this usually consists of the bride's parents if they are hosting the occasion, the groom's parents and the bride and groom. In most cases where the entrance hall of the reception venue permits a large number of people to stand around and wait until they are announced by the toastmaster, and providing that there are no more than a hundred guests, the receiving line may be as follows:

## The Receiving Line

1  Best Man (if Toastmaster    4. Groom's Mother
   is not available)           5. Groom's Father
2. Bride's Mother              6. Bride
3  Bride's Father              7. Groom

The lady in each couple will receive the guests before her husband.

If it is a very formal wedding where a toastmaster is provided to announce the arrival of the guests as they arrive at the door, you and the chief bridesmaid may be expected to join the end of the receiving line. If a toastmaster is not provided, this full receiving line can be rather pointless, you can be more usefully employed acting as toastmaster and mingling, ensuring the smooth passage of guests. Even when there is a large number of guests the bride and groom have been known to receive them on their own.

At this point it should be mentioned that it is absolutely vital for the best man to memorise the names of at least the people most concerned with the wedding whom he will be talking to and about at the reception, however bewildering he may find the sea of faces. If you are not good at remembering names, it is a good idea to write down and memorise, before the reception, the names of the members of the wedding party. (The checklists at the back of the book should prove helpful.)

At a formal occasion, you may be asked to fulfil the toastmaster's role of announcing the guests but at most weddings you would simply be making sure that people enter in an orderly way, showing them where they can leave their coats and greeting as many people as possible by name.

At an informal reception it is not necessary to have a toastmaster or a receiving line. The bride and groom may simply greet their guests together at the door and let them mingle freely. If the greeting of guests is dispensed with entirely, the bride and groom must be sure to thank each guest before the reception comes to a close.

The guests will be given an aperitif when they

have been received by the bride and groom. When the last guest has taken his drink the toastmaster will call for attention and direct everyone to their appointed seats. After the main course, come the speeches followed by the cake-cutting ceremony and then coffee is served.

## · DISPLAY OF WEDDING GIFTS ·

Fortunately the custom of displaying wedding gifts at the wedding reception seems to be less popular than it was at one time. If you are in a position to offer advice to the bride or her parents about this point out that it could be asking for trouble. Whereas one would never suspect the motives of guests or venue staff, it is simply impossible to check on everyone else who may be wandering around the premises. Any light-fingered member of the community has a golden opportunity to see what spoils there are for the taking in the couple's new home and any professional criminal will have no difficulty in finding out their address.

The other argument against the display of wedding gifts is that some people who could only afford a bread board might be rather embarrassed to see it nestling against a canteen of solid silver cutlery, particularly if name tags accompany the gifts. The bride may display gifts at home before the wedding. Hopefully then, the bride will have received most gifts before the reception.

However efficiently the wedding gifts have been dealt with, there will still be some people who will turn up at the reception with carefully wrapped odd and awkward looking shapes containing such things as gardening tools and waste-paper bins, not easily sent by post or too late to pass on before the day. A table behind the receiving line will avoid the likelihood of juggling parcels while trying to greet guests. The bridesmaids could help out here to ensure that labels are stuck to and remain on the right gifts. You should then take charge and ensure their security for the duration of the reception.

## · WEDDING BREAKFAST ·

This does not mean that the meal must take place in the morning – it is simply the term used for a sit-down meal. In addition to place name cards, an overall seating plan is usually prepared so that guests know the general location of their seats as they enter the dining room.

The main wedding party sits along one side of a long table facing the guests, ensuring that everyone can view the top table. The bride and groom sit in the middle; the groom always sits on the right of the bride and other males and females are alternated. Although top table seating will vary according to the circumstances, there is always a place for the best man.

When a divorce has occurred in a family, the seating arrangements will depend on how amicable everyone concerned is prepared to be for this occasion. The greatest bone of contention arises when the bride's parents have been divorced and the bride has been brought up by her mother and possibly a stepfather. If the bride's own father has remarried and for the purposes of the wedding has asked if he may give away his daughter at the wedding ceremony, it may be more appropriate for him to be given a place at the top table together with his wife.

A seating plan must be tactful; all the people concerned must be approached by the bride and their agreement sought.

If the bride's father gave her away at the wedding ceremony, the courtesy of making the first speech could be extended to her stepfather. Remember that the stepfather will probably have played a large and loving part in the bride's life: this is one way of expressing gratitude. If this should be the case, he could take his seat next to the bride at the top table.

After the bride and groom have had time to circulate among their guests, and any extra photographs have been taken, or, in the case of a sit-down reception the final course has been finished, the toastmaster will call order for the cake-cutting ceremony and the speeches, or vice versa. If the cake is cut first, it is whipped away by the catering staff to be cut up for the guests to eat with their coffee. The toastmaster will then announce the speeches. At large formal wedding receptions, a toastmaster is usually provided and most venues are able to offer this service. A toastmaster can contribute greatly to the smooth running of the reception, beginning his duties by announcing the guests as they arrive and move towards the receiving line. He then calls the guests to their seats when the meal is ready for serving. He announces the person who is to say grace. If the minister is present, he must be asked to say grace. Otherwise, including or omitting grace is a matter for the family to decide and may depend on their own religious beliefs, but it is in keeping with the spirit of a church wedding. When everyone is

# THE BEST BEST MAN

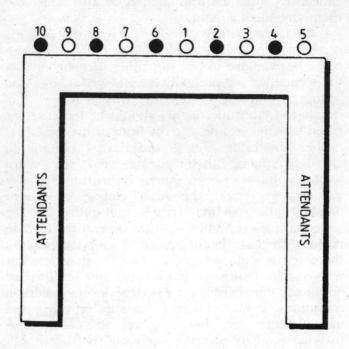

## *Top Table Seating*

1  Bride
2. Bride's Father
3  Groom's Mother
4. Minister
5. Chief Bridesmaid

6. Groom
7. Bride's Mother
8. Groom's Father
9. Minister's Wife
10. Best Man

# THE RECEPTION

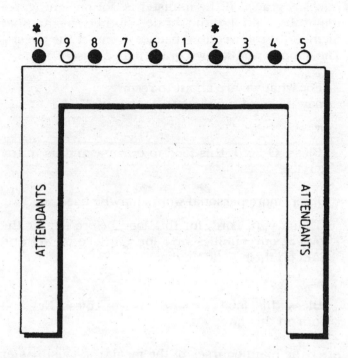

## Top table seating in special circumstances

1  Bride
2. Bride's Father*
3  Groom's Mother
4. Best Man
5. Bride's Stepmother

6. Groom
7. Bride's Mother
8. Groom's Father
9. Chief Bridesmaid
10. Bride's Stepfather*

*Whoever is proposing the first toast should sit next to the Bride.

seated, the toastmaster should announce: "Ladies and gentlemen, the Reverend Martin Massey will now say grace." If the minister is not present, grace might be said by the bride's father, by another member of the wedding party, or one of the guests. The simple, well-known grace may be used:

"For what we are about to receive,
may the Lord make us truly thankful"

or:

"Bless, O Lord, this food to our use and us to thy service."

Other, more personal words may be used, e.g:

"Thank you, Lord, for this food before us, for the love of our families and for the love of Nel and Sam on their wedding day."

or:

"Bless this food, O Lord, as you bless Nel and Sam on this happy day."

After the main courses of the meal, the toastmaster formally calls upon each of the speakers to propose the toasts following which, at the coffee stage, he calls for order for the cutting of the cake ceremony, if not previously dealt with. He announces: "Ladies and gentlemen may I have your attention please. The bride and groom will now cut the cake."

Later, he announces the departure of the bride and groom.

In the absence of a professional toastmaster, the best man, a relative or one of the guests who has a

THE RECEPTION

resounding voice and a confident manner, can fulfil
these tasks. It is, of course, essential that the
person is fully briefed well in advance of the day.

## · SPEECHES ·

"Ladies and gentlemen, silence please for the bride's
father" (or close friend of the family).

The bride's father, first in to bat, will thank
everyone for coming to the wedding and say a few
words of welcome to his new son-in-law. He
concludes by proposing a toast to the health of the
bride and groom.

The groom will reply on behalf of his new bride
and himself, thanking the first speaker for the
toast, the guests for coming to the wedding and for
their gifts. He may thank the best man for all his
good deeds and present him with a small gift as a
token of thanks. He concludes his speech by
proposing a toast to the bridesmaids.

The best man will reply on behalf of the bridesmaids. He will congratulate the groom on his good luck
and proceed to read the telegrams (which he must
check beforehand to weed out any dubious ones).

After these formalities the bride and groom will retire
to their room to change into their going-away clothes.

The reception discussed earlier deals with an
average formal reception where the venue catering
staff undertake all the catering arrangements.
There exists a much more formal celebration which
includes a dance or disco in the evening, and, at
the other end of the scale, there is a simple
gathering of friends, with a small buffet, usually
held at the home of the bride's parents.

## · ENTERTAINMENT ·

A wedding reception which includes a dance or disco will usually start with a wedding celebration held as late in the afternoon as possible. Guests will often arrive at the wedding dressed in their formal evening attire, with the exception of the main members of the wedding party who will wear formal morning clothes and wedding attire.

When the formalities are over the tables are pushed back or guests will move to another room and the toastmaster will announce that dancing will commence. The bride and groom lead the dancing followed by the chief bridesmaid and the best man, members of the two families and finally the guests. The best man should be one of the first to ask the bride to dance. During the evening you should dance with all the ladies in the wedding party and as many of the female guests as possible. You should make yourself generally helpful in making sure that everyone enjoys themselves by serving drinks or sending waitresses to people who need serving, chatting and being sociable.

## · THE SIMPLE RECEPTION ·

This sometimes, but not always, follows a registry office wedding. If the couple are to be married on a Saturday the wedding must take place in the morning. Facilities for large numbers at a registry office are rare and guests invited to such a ceremony will often include families and close friends only.

The wedding is sometimes followed by an informal lunch at a restaurant and the guests will disperse to prepare for a larger reception held in the evening, perhaps at a hotel. There is no reason why the guest list for the reception should be restricted in any way.

For the smaller gathering, many catering firms are able to provide their services at private houses and supply both the food and all the necessary equipment, but if the catering is to be carried out by the bride's family the best man's duties before this type of reception may be far more complicated. He will probably be expected to help with the collection of various pieces of equipment: glasses and delicacies. He may be expected to take charge of the drinks for the evening. He may be asked to organise the musical entertainments for the evening! If a barman is not part of the 'reception package', the groom should have someone other than a member of the wedding party who will act in this role, or a number of people to help out. It would be inappropriate to expect the best man to spend the reception behind the bar when he should be enjoying the occasion with the guests. However, if the best man does find himself in this position, in return for all this he may expect to be let off the ordeal of making a wedding speech, but even an informal celebration will require a few words of congratulation. A stand-up buffet-type reception demands no formal seating arrangements except that the bridal party should have a formal table where they can be served. At the end of the evening, the best man may also be required to help with the washing up!

## · CAR DECORATIONS ·

During the course of the wedding reception someone is bound to organise a sabotage party for the going-away car, especially if it is the couple's own vehicle. Unless you can take the precaution of hiding the car two miles down the road, this is an inevitable wedding day ritual. Hopefully, no one would ever be foolish enough to interfere with the car's machinery but it is up to you to ensure that this does not happen.

## · DEPARTURE ·

If the groom is using his car, the best man will collect the groom's car keys and luggage and drive the car around to the front door. He should hand over any documents which he has been keeping for the groom, plus the telegrams which can be read once again at the couple's leisure if they wish, otherwise they may be handed to the bride's mother for safe keeping until their return from honeymoon.

The bride and groom will return to the reception room to spend a little time with their guests and the chief bridesmaid should return the bouquet to the bride.

Led by the bride and groom, the families and guests will congregate ready for their departure. A last round of good-byes and congratulations, then the bride will throw her bouquet to the next matrimonial victim and the couple will drive away in a flurry of confetti!

The guests will slowly begin to disperse at an appropriate time.

Together with the chief bridesmaid you should

collect from the changing room, the couple's wedding clothes and wedding gifts. Ask the bride's parents if they need help to transport the gifts. If there has been a sit-down reception, collect some napkins, place cards and other mementoes, which the bride may like to keep on her return from the honeymoon. The bride's mother will collect the rest of the wedding cake from the catering staff, to be sent around to people who could not attend the wedding. The top tier of the cake can be used for a future special occasion such as a christening, since wedding cake will keep fresh for years in an air-tight container. Be sure to thank the staff for their help, on behalf of the bride and groom, and take the couple's belongings around to the home of the bride's parents.

Finally, congratulate yourself, and the chief bridesmaid, on a job well done!

## · AFTER THE WEDDING ·

Remember that if the groom hired a morning suit it must be returned as soon as possible.

You could visit the couple's new home before they return from their honeymoon, to leave vases of flowers or suggest this to the chief bridesmaid. A small thought like this makes a wonderful home-coming.

# · 10 ·
# *The Best Man's Speech*

If you are just an ordinary guy with no aspirations to politics or anything else that involves public speaking, the idea of having to stand up in front of an audience and entertain them at a wedding will probably colour your thoughts blue for weeks before the big day, and yet there is absolutely no need for this to be an ordeal with a little planning, forethought and a few basic guidelines. Very few people are practised 'after dinner' speakers and there is no need to worry as every speech maker is nervous. In any case, it is not difficult to make a speech to an audience already warmed up by the happiness of the occasion. They do not expect, or want, a long and important serious oratory! They simply expect a few sincere and perhaps amusing words from speakers and the toasts so that they can get on with really enjoying themselves. It should be remembered that the speeches are not the most important part of the wedding and if the speaker loses his nerve, he need only say a few words of thanks, congratulations and good wishes.

The purpose of wedding speeches are threefold: to congratulate the couple and wish them well in their future life together; to thank appropriate people; and to propose a toast.

They occur after the meal and are usually

followed by the cake-cutting ceremony. Following each toast, all guests should stand, raise their glasses, repeat the toast and drink to whoever mentioned.

# · ORDER OF SPEECHES · AND TOASTS

Speeches at wedding receptions include the toasts. Each speaker should be announced briefly by the toastmaster or the best man.

## First Toast
The first toast is made by the giver-away (usually the bride's father) who stands and says a few words about the bride and groom before proposing the toast which is to the health of the bride and groom.

## Reply to the First Toast
The groom responds on behalf of the bride and himself.

## Second Toast
Following on, the groom proposes the toast to the bridesmaids.

## Reply to the Second Toast
The best man replies on behalf of the bridesmaids, gives a speech and reads out any messages and telegrams. (If there are no bridesmaids, the best man need not speak at all. It really is a matter of personal choice.) To conclude, the best man announces the cutting of the cake.

No other speeches are made at formal weddings, but at more informal receptions the bride herself is sometimes asked to say a few words.

A practised and witty speaker may make a second proposal of health to the newly-weds but this is fairly unusual.

## · METHOD ·

Unless extremely accomplished in delivering speeches on the spur of the moment, plans should be made in advance.

There are various ways of presenting a speech:

- Read the speech from notes
- Recite the speech from memory
- Refer to brief 'headline' notes which serve as memory-joggers for previously studied text.

The first method is disastrous in that the speech will sound like a public announcement, it will be unnatural and lacking in liveliness and spontaneity. It also leaves little or no opportunity for mentioning unexpected events of the day. Consequently, it is not a good idea to write out the speech and read it word for word, since it will not come over well and will put the audience to sleep in no time.

Similarly, if the speech is recited from memory, it too is inflexible as it prohibits comment on some little incident of the day such as the black cat that crossed the bride's path that morning. The speech may also sound like an audition before the local amateur dramatics society. There is also the problem of what to do with your hands!

# THE BEST MAN'S SPEECH

The third method is a compromise, used by many public speakers, and seems to produce the best results in that the speech will have shape and will include all the main points which should not be forgotten. It is perhaps the best option for a wedding speech and also has the advantage of giving the speaker something to do with his hands!

It will have been carefully planned and will possess the flexibility for improvisation when delivered. It is these last-minute additions which can really bring a speech to life. The headers (written on cards) allow the addition of amusing comments or development of the material as best suits the occasion.

When the wording of the speech is finalised and sounds natural, key (memory) words should be highlighted and transferred to plain post cards – a separate word written boldly on each card followed by a few memory-joggers. Each of the cards should then be numbered so that they remain in the correct sequence. The cards should state the things that must be included, for example:

- thank groom for the toast to the bridesmaids
- congratulations to the happy couple
- and now to the telegrams
- and now to the cutting of the cake

The things that should be said may then be added, perhaps the recollection of an incident about the couple which would make an amusing story. The cards can be held in front of you and can be flipped from the front to the back of the pile during natural pauses ready for the next prompt. Cards are more manageable and do not flap and crumple like paper. They look professional and can be hidden in a pocket until needed. It is probable that several drafts will be necessary until the wording and order take the shape of a reasonable and structured speech. The first draft should be discarded for a few days – a fresh reassessment will work wonders!

# · PRESENTATION ·

## Practice
The fact that the speaker has not spoken in public before is no cause for worry. A couple of timed practice runs in front of a mirror or, even better, a video, and perhaps the comments of a close but critical friend, will allow the speaker to hear how well the items run together and will aid confidence. Sometimes a seemingly good and logical flow of composition appears to flow on paper but does not work when spoken. A tape recorder, or the video of course, can be used to check for verbal idiosyncrasies. Some people use certain phrases repeatedly without realising: for example, "you know", "like", "sort of", "um", "er"!

## Delivery
The secret of good delivery is to take control of the audience from the very first moment by being confident with an easy relaxed manner. The audience will feel reassured enough to relax comfortably and enjoy the speech.

There will always be a babble of comments between speeches as well as the scraping of chairs and fidgeting as people get comfortable. This time can be used to take a few relaxing deep breaths, and to cast a glance through the speech notes.

## Speech Manner
The way a speech is spoken is very important. It is easy to sound pompous and/or patronizing when speaking on your feet but on the other hand, too much informality should also be avoided. Even a highly informal reception is an important occasion and the manner of the speeches should reflect this fact. The speaker must judge for himself an appropriate manner. The audience will almost certainly be made up of known family and friends and some strangers. These strangers should be borne in mind and will not expect an address that is too familiar. It should be remembered that guests at a wedding are there to enjoy themselves and they will be tolerant of inexperienced speakers but not rude or over familiar ones.

## Formal Words, Phrases and Clichés
Generally speaking, these should be avoided as they will sound either boring or pompous, or both!

## Slang
The use of slang should be avoided as it detracts from that 'sense of occasion' and also because some listeners will be left in the dark, particularly those who are too young or too old to understand modern slang usage.

## Swearing
The speaker must not be tempted to swear. Even a "damn" or "blast" can offend, so swearing must be avoided at all costs.

## Pronunciation

A natural accent should be used. It is foolish to assume a 'stage' voice or put on a refined, posh accent if this does not come naturally. Regional differences in accent and pronunciation are nothing about which to be ashamed. The guests expect and should be talked to in a similar way that the speaker would talk to a family friend who had called in to visit.

On the other hand, sloppy pronunciation should be avoided. It is worth noting the fact that consonants at the ends of words can get lost when spoken, especially when the next word starts with another consonant. For example, when saying 'that time' or 'and did', there should be a tiny pause between the words. The best way to avoid this particular pitfall, which is good advice to many inexperienced speakers, is to speak just a little more slowly than normal.

## Voice Level

Everyone knows the old advice to speakers: "Stand up, speak up and shut up". A speaker's voice simply must be heard, or there is no point in making a speech at all. Speak clearly but not so loudly that you could shatter a pane of glass at ten paces and not as though someone is standing on your windpipe.

Nervousness often makes a speaker inaudible – so does an unaccustomedly large room and it can be foolish to assume that a microphone will improve matters! The technique of using a microphone must be practised if it is to be of benefit and if this is impossible, the advice of an experienced user should be sought. It is also important to ensure that there is someone on hand who will know what to do if the system misbehaves as prompt action will be necessary to avoid a most embarrassing pause in the proceedings. Microphones tend to create a distance between speaker and audience and are perhaps best forgotten for a wedding speech.

Another point the speaker should remember is never try to compete with extraneous noise. When a speaker first stands up there is usually a continuing babble of conversation, perhaps the clinking of glasses being put down, or the clattering of chairs being rearranged to face the speaker. The speaker must wait until all noise has died down and the listeners' full attention is attracted before commencement. When all is quiet, the speaker should jump straight into the speech, perhaps with a witty remark so that the audience responds and is eager for more. The voice needs to be projected so that it is heard by those at the back of the room. Deep breaths and natural pauses will help.

## Duration

Speeches must be brief and should be timed to take no more than five minutes at the outside. Consider how you feel about speeches made at a social function. Do you sit up brimming with interest and expectancy, or do you think: "Oh no – the speeches – I hope they don't go on for too long"? If you are honest your thoughts will tend to the latter and if speeches are short, concise and sincere, then you are probably agreeably surprised!

Breathing time must be allowed! This may sound obvious but when a speaker is nervous, there is a tendency to hold breath unintentionally. A few practice runs will facilitate relaxation and help to give a good presentation.

## Pace

The one thing that a novice speaker forgets is to breathe! In normal conversation there is hardly any need for extra breathing effort to make oneself heard and conversation is normally a dialogue where rests occur between exchanges. Yet for the speech maker there are no such pauses, unless these are deliberately made. The best advice is not to hurry, taking a leisurely pace and pausing between sentences or even between phrases.

## Posture

The speaker should position his feet slightly apart and should stand upright but relaxed in a natural posture. This aids comfort and gives an air of confidence. There are certain things which nervous first time speakers do unconsciously and which should be avoided at all costs at they distract and irritate the audience:

- clinking loose change or keys in pockets
- mopping the face or brow with a handkerchief
- shuffling from one foot to the other as if doing the cha-cha!
- rocking backwards and forwards
- easing tie away from shirt collar as if on trial for life!

## Gestures

A lively manner does improve speech delivery but the inexperienced speaker should avoid making gestures to illustrate speech unless they come absolutely naturally, otherwise they will look posed and peculiar. There is nothing worse than watching a speaker flinging his arms around like an orchestra conductor. It detracts from the speech and there can be few people who can concentrate on the words when the speaker appears to be trying to swat a mosquito! Some speakers grip their coat lapels, but this tends to give them the appearance of a racecourse bookmaker shouting the odds. Others lay their hands palm down on the table and rest their weight on them, giving the stance of a shopkeeper waiting for a customer! From the point of view of good manners, it would perhaps be unforgivable to stand with hands in pockets, but if this is the only way that a speaker can feel happy and by feeling comfortable can deliver a good speech, then perhaps it *is* forgivable.

The best advice is to try to be as natural as possible avoiding irritating gestures. Even if prompt cards are not referred to, they do provide something to do with your hands. An accomplished speaker stands with his hands loosely at his side and gestures naturally as appropriate but this is very difficult for the beginner to achieve. Again, practising in front of a mirror is a good way of assessing gestures and performance. A drink of water will satisfy a dry throat during the speech; a little alcohol stimulates and relaxes, whereas several drinks slow down the thought processes and have a disastrous effect on speech making ability, so it is vital that the speaker restricts himself to just one or two drinks beforehand.

## Vision

The speaker should not look at floors, walls or ceilings, he should look in the general direction of the audience and towards the subject of the toast when proposing, without staring fixedly causing embarrassment.

## Summary of Points to Remember:

1 Plan speech and write bold 'headliners' on small cards organised in small sections and number the pages
2 Rehearse speech
3 Dress unobtrusively, e.g. avoid anything that jangles
4 Stand still, comfortably relaxed and upright with feet slightly apart
5 Speak clearly but not so loudly that you could shatter a pane of glass at ten paces and not as though someone is standing on your windpipe
6 Never clink the loose change in your pocket
7 Never shuffle your feet as though you are practising the cha-cha
8 Never ease your tie away from your collar – you are not on trial for your life
9 Do not mop your face with a handkerchief – you are not about to pass out
10 Do not compete with noise but wait for silence
11 Hold the cards in your hand or hold hands behind your back
12 Take a deep relaxing breath before commencing and remember to breathe throughout the speech
13 Be flexible if there is something amusing to add and if this suits the plan

14 Look at the audience as you speak but not with a fixed stare

15 Speak slowly and clearly, varying speed and voice levels slightly

16 Keep the tone conversational

17 Remember that the audience is not critical – they are there to enjoy themselves; to eat, talk and congratulate the bride and groom

18 Be brief –
3 minutes is ample; 5 minutes is maximum and 6 is too long. Consider how *you* feel about speeches made at a social function

19 Do not say, "Unaccustomed as I am to public speaking ..."

20 Do not use unnecessarily long words or sentences

21 Do not use formal words or phrases not normally used

22 Do not blaspheme, use slang, tell lies, be pompous or patronising

23 Be appropriate, to the point and sincere

24 Avoid embarrassing stories, do not mention anything sensitive

25 Be careful of telling jokes, make fun only of yourself

26 Do not forget to respond to and propose the toast

27 Ensure that there is a glass of water at hand

28 Limit the number of drinks before your speech

## · CONTENT ·

Like every properly constructed speech, a wedding speech must have a beginning, a middle and an end. A speaker might start by saying that he has never made a speech before, or with the carefully chosen joke or a short amusing story. This will immediately set a pleasantly relaxed tone and ensure that the audience is really attentive. When it comes to the serious content of the speech, it is important to remember that this is the response to and the proposal of the toast. When responding to the toast, the wording can be informal but it must be made clear in the opening sentence that the speaker is thanking the company for drinking the speaker's health. A simple "Thank you very much" is often surprisingly effective, or "I thank you most sincerely for your kind wishes ... It was most kind of you to drink to the bridesmaids." When proposing the toast, wording should be a little more formal: the speaker simply says, at the end of his speech, "I ask you to rise and drink the health of ..." or similar words. It is advisable to use plain conversational English and to make it grammatically correct. Archaic expressions such as "Please be upstanding" are no longer necessary. To conclude a speech, it is quite acceptable to repeat the thanks for the toast that has been drunk, thus avoiding any need to devise a clever and obvious ending.

The best man's speech needs to be lighter in tone than those of the bride's father and the groom and should cover the following:

1 Thank the groom for the toast on behalf of the bridesmaids and generally add a few complimentary remarks of your own. Thank anyone who has helped you to do the job properly, or anyone the bride has asked you to thank specially.

2 Offer your congratulations to the bride and groom and offer some thoughts (hopes) for their future. These can be amusing but never of a risqué nature. You may add a story about how the couple first met or some suitable amusing anecdote. It is often useful to use an amusing anecdote or quotation at this point to ensure the full attention of the audience.

3 You may propose a toast to absent friends if important guests have been unable to attend the wedding.

4 Introduce and read any telegrams from absent friends, remembering that there may be children and maiden aunts present. (You should have vetted these beforehand and excluded any hint of vulgarity from the public recital.) It is acceptable to group together several telegrams which convey the same wording, merely announcing the common message and the names of the senders.

5 Introduce the cutting of the cake.

Your speech will be preceded first by that of the bride's father, who will formally thank everyone for coming to the wedding and welcome his new son-in-law to the family. He will conclude by proposing a toast to the bride and groom.

The groom will then reply on behalf of himself and the bride. He will thank the guests for the good wishes and wedding gifts. He should thank his father-in-law for both his daughter's hand and for his toast. He will conclude by proposing a toast to the bridesmaids if there are any. If not, he may well propose the health of the bride's parents and his own in thanks for all their help over the years and for such a splendid wedding.

Your speech will follow.

There is really no need for the bride to make a speech and she is seldom expected to do so. However the custom is growing for the bride to say just a very few words if she wishes – three or four sentences to thank her husband are sufficient. Sometimes the bride speaks immediately after her husband has responded to the toast to the two of them, but if he is proposing the toast to the bridesmaids, this is difficult as he has to rise again after the bride to propose the toast. Consequently this is not really satisfactory and to remedy this, it is better that someone else proposes the toast to the bridesmaids. The best man sometimes introduces the bride and again the order of speakers will need consideration in advance. In any case, the best man's response usually concludes the speeches when he announces the time for the cutting of the cake.

## Comic Stories and Jokes

The art of wit cannot be acquired in a few weeks of practice; nor can anyone be expected to do a good job with someone else's script written specially for the occasion. Remember you are not a television comedian. A professional comedian's success lies in the ability to act, in facial expression and in the confidence that comes with assured popularity and perfect timing. Few ordinary people possess this talent. If you are among the lucky ones who do you will be well aware of your ability and will need little, if any, guidance. However if you are not, you are best advised not to attempt a witty speech as the result will, almost certainly, be painful and boring. Taking jokes from a book could be a disaster, because the chances are that the punch line will be forgotten or that it will be badly recited and people will not laugh. Remember that nothing falls flatter than a joke which no one understands or thinks is funny.

There was a time when it was considered improper to recall a single joke or an amusing story in the course of a wedding speech. Today, at all but the most formal receptions, a humorous anecdote is quite acceptable provided that it is of the kind that could be told to the vicar, or an elderly maiden aunt – there must be no hint of the blue or the risqué for fear of embarrassing the bride and groom or the guests. So, references to honeymoons, wedding nights, any previous marriage or liaisons, future family, sex and the like are out. However tempted you may be, never mention all the hundreds of girl friends who have figured in the groom's life. Jokes that are witty, innocent or affectionate may all be suitable for wedding speeches. Mild jokes about nagging wives and lazy husbands are permissible provided that they are followed by a disclaimer making it clear that the jokes relate in no way to the bride and groom. Making jokes at the expense of the bride or her mother are unforgivable but making jokes at one's own expense is a good way of interesting and maintaining the attention of the audience, for example a comment about the speaker's shyness, and his inadequacy as a public speaker. So, there is no reason why one suitable joke should not be voiced as this does help to relax both speaker and audience. One-liners are often safer and more effective than long jokes and funny stories. The best man's speech traditionally includes humorous references and it is vital that these are pitched correctly. Funny stories or anecdotes should flow naturally into the speech and not be slotted in for their own sake, for example:

> "This splendid turn-out reminds me of the time I attended ... I heard a very good story there and since I'm not above a little light larceny, I shall tell it to you as my own ... ."

or:

> "What excellent champagne. It makes me think of a friend of mine who drank too much of the stuff and ... ."

One short joke is sufficient as there is nothing more boring than the speaker who fancies himself as a comedian and relates a string of "funnies".

The boring speech comes as a result of trying to prepare a cleverly contrived oration. To a captive audience this is precisely how such a speech will sound: contrived, often flat and in many cases far too long. Comic stories, anecdotes and jokes need to be relevant to the speech in some way.

Above all, it is the sincere speech that people want to hear at a wedding. It is unlikely to fail because it explains exactly how you feel and no one should object to this providing you do not go on for too long.

## Second Marriages

Speeches and toasts at a woman's second marriage are subtly different from those at first weddings. The toast to the bride and groom may still be given by the bride's father, but this is fairly unusual. He is not, after all, giving his daughter away in marriage this time! Normally this toast will be made by a male friend, perhaps the husband of the bride's woman friend who sent the invitations for her, or the toast may be made by the best man, if there is one. There are sometimes only two speeches: the proposal of the new couple's health and the bridegroom's response. These speeches will probably not have the same lightness and gaiety as at a first marriage as the tone needs to be a little more serious. It must be remembered that it is bad form to refer to the bride's earlier marriage. If you are best man at a wedding following a previous divorce, or if either of the couple is widowed and have to make a speech, do not make any references whatsoever to the past marriage and certainly never say anything like "Better luck this time" – you are supposed to be tactful, remember!

## Sample Speeches

Typical best man's speeches could run along the following lines:

Ladies and gentlemen,
on behalf of the bridesmaids, I should like to thank Sam for his toast, and I must say that I'm really enjoying myself – the opportunity of being surrounded by a gathering of pretty women doesn't happen every day. It's a pity we're only allowed one bride – I'd marry them all if I could – and if they'd have me!

A lot has been said about the bride today, and I would like to say some more! She looks absolutely gorgeous and she's a fabulous person too. Sam's a very lucky guy – he's looking so smug and pleased with himself that he doesn't really need any congratulations. Perhaps some of you don't know how all this started.

Well – Sam was at a party and he tried to phone me to ask where I'd got to. Instead of me he got a wrong number and Nel was on the other end and after a long conversation, he asked her for a date ... need I say more? – except that I wish it was me who made that phone call – I've never had such good fortune.

Sam may not think he needs any congratulations, but I'm going to wish them both all the luck in the world anyway, and I'm sure everyone will agree that this has been a great wedding.

Now, I have to read some of the telegrams:

"Hoping you two never get your wires crossed again"

Love Tom and Jenny

"Best wishes for the future"

Love from Penny and Paul

etc. etc.

I think that's probably enough for now – if I read them all we'll still be here next week and these two have a plane to catch. Once again Sam and Nel – all the very best and a long and happy life to you.

Ladies and gentlemen,
I am called the best man, but goodness knows why, for no-one pays much attention to a man in my position today. They all say, "Isn't the bride radiant?" and "Doesn't the groom look dashing?"

and "How pretty the bridesmaids are!" But you never hear anyone say, "What a fine figure of a man the Best Man is!" If they notice me at all they think I'm one of the caterers! But enough about me. I am standing up at the moment to speak for the bridesmaids, to say thank you on their behalf for the kind things Sam said about them. To tell you the truth I don't think he did them justice, but then that's understandable on a day like this. I'm surprised he even noticed that they were there at all, the way he's been looking at Nel. Never mind, I'm still a bachelor and my judgement is emotionally unclouded, and I think they're the finest looking set of bridesmaids I've ever seen. I can see that you all agree with me. So on behalf of the bridesmaids, thank you very much indeed.

Ladies and gentlemen,
I feel a little strange replying to the toast to the bridesmaids, because, as you can all see, I am not a bridesmaid! It is, however a very pleasant job because I think we all feel that Sam was absolutely right in saying such nice things about them. I would like to thank him for saying nice things about me, too, though I must admit I do rather deserve them. I mean, where would a bridegroom be without his best man? The friend at hand when panic grips him on the very steps of the church. The reassuring voice in his ear when he is absolutely sure he has forgotten some vital detail in his honeymoon arrangements. The wise counsellor who knows just how everything should be done on the most important day in a man's life. I felt sure that Sam had picked me for

this important job because he had weighed up my fine qualities and thought me ideal. And while we were sitting in church waiting for Nel to arrive I did ask him to confirm this. Do you know what he said? He says, "Oh, well, Eric is in the Middle East right now and I thought you might just about manage." Never mind, I forgive him. The only thing I find it hard to forgive him for is marrying this beautiful young woman, who must surely have preferred me had Sam given her the opportunity to get to know me a little better. Let me add my good wishes to this handsome couple, and let me say thank you most sincerely on behalf of the bridesmaids.

## Quotations

You have to be careful about including quotations into a speech, for if you use more than two you can sound awfully pompous. However, quotations are useful in that they set you thinking, they start a train of thought which can make the thread of a speech and if you can find just one quotation that is especially apt to the particular circumstances of the wedding, by all means use it. If you do use more than one quotation, make it clear that you have looked it up and tell the audience where the quotations came from. In other words, do not make a parade of learning. Throw in your quotation lightly and develop it to suit the circumstances. Say something like:

I would pretend that these splendid literary quotations I am giving you came straight out of memory. I *would* pretend – that is if Sam hadn't seen me thumbing through my book of quotations last week.

or:

Let me confess I had never heard that quotation until yesterday. Someone suggested it to me, and it seemed so apt I have to pass it on to you today. Though this is such a highly intellectual gathering that I am sure you all knew it anyway!

or:

There used to be a popular song which had this refrain, if I remember properly: "Love makes the world go round." Any schoolboy will tell you that the world goes round because it can't stop spinning. But looking at Nel and Sam today, I think it is perfectly true to say that love makes *their* world go round ...

or:

You all know the old song: "Why am I always the bridesmaid, never the blushing bride?" Well I feel like changing it a little and singing: "Why am I always the best man, never the blushing bridegroom?" Because this is the third wedding at which I've been best man in eighteen months; if it goes on like this I shall lose my amateur status. Between you and me, I can tell you the real reason why I'm on the shelf at thirty and that is that I've never met a girl like Nel ...

So, quotations, like jokes, can be adapted to suit the circumstances and can add purpose and shape to a speech and as long as they are dropped in as the source of an idea.

111

There follows a number of useful quotations, grouped under the headings of 'Marriage', 'Love' and 'Various'.

Some of these quotations are not quite flattering about the institution of marriage – indeed some are positively cynical – and it will be obvious that many writers had a jaded view of marriage, so it is important to choose something that will not offend. If the more jaded views are used they must be qualified by a denial of the truth of their sentiments, e.g. "Anyone would find it impossible to hold such views in the presence of such obvious wedded bliss".


## *Marriage*

For every marriage then is best in tune,
When that the wife is May, the husband's June.
ROWLAND WATKYNS

Hanging and marriage, you know, go by destiny.
GEORGE FARQUHAR

Is not marriage an open question, when it is alleged from the beginning of the world, that such as are in the institution wish to get out, and such that are out wish to get in.
RALPH WALDO EMERSON

Marriage is a wonderful institution,
but who wants to live in an institution?
GROUCHO MARX

## THE BEST MAN'S SPEECH

It won't be a stylish marriage,
I can't afford a carriage.

HARRY DACRE

Marriage has many pains,
but celibacy has no pleasures.

Marriages would in general be as happy, and often
more so, if they were all made by the Lord
Chancellor.

DR SAMUEL JOHNSON

Marriage is nothing but a civil contract.

JOHN SELDEN

Marriage is a sort of friendship recognized by the
police.

No woman should marry a teetotaller.

To marry is to domesticate the Recording Angel.
Once you have married there is nothing left for you,
not even suicide, but to be good.

Times are changed with him who married; there are
no more by-path meadows, where you may
innocently linger, but the road lies long and
straight and dusty to the grave.

In marriage a man becomes slack and selfish, and
undergoes a fatty degeneration of his moral being.

Marriage is like life in this: that it is a field of battle
not a bed of roses.

# THE BEST BEST MAN

Marriage is a step so grave and decisive that it attracts light-headed, variable men by its very awfulness.

ROBERT LOUIS STEVENSON

It is a woman's business to get married as soon as possible, and a man's to keep unmarried as long as possible.

Marriage is popular because it combines the maximum of temptation with the maximum of opportunity.

GEORGE BERNARD SHAW

Marriage the happiest bond of love might be,
If hands were only joined when hearts agree.

GEORGE GRANVILLE

Though marriage makes man and wife one flesh,
it leaves 'em two fools.

WILLIAM CONGREVE

For in what stupid age or nation,
Was marriage ever out of fashion?

SAMUEL BUTLER

When I said I would die a bachelor, I did not think I should live till I were married.

Let me not, to the marriage of true minds,
Admit impediments.

God, the best maker of all marriages,
Combine your hearts in one.

WILLIAM SHAKESPEARE

# THE BEST MAN'S SPEECH

St. Aldegonde had a taste for marriages and public cxccutions.

BENJAMIN DISRAELI

The reason why so few marriages are happy is because young ladies spend their time in making nets, not in making cages.

JONATHAN SWIFT

One fool at least, in every married couple.

HENRY FIELDING

Love and marriage,
Love and marriage,
Go together like a horse and carriage.

POPULAR SONG

Strange to say what delight we married people have to see these poor fools decoyed into our condition.

SAMUEL PEPYS

Married in haste, we may repent at leisure.

WILLIAM CONGREVE

I am to be married within these three days:
married past redemption.

JOHN DRYDEN

I have always thought that every woman should marry and no man.

BENJAMIN DISRAELI

He is dreadfully married. He's the most married man I ever saw in my life.

ARTEMUS WARD

# THE BEST BEST MAN

Wen you're a married man, Samivel, you'll understand a good many things as you don't understand now; but vether it's worth while going through so much to learn so little, as the charity boy said ven he got to the end of the alphabet, is a matter o'taste.

SAM WELLER
(in Dickens' *Pickwick Papers*)

Advice to persons about to marry – don't.

PUNCH 1845

Remember it's easy to marry a rich woman as a poor woman.

This I set down as a positive truth:
a woman with fair opportunities and without a positive hump, may marry whom she likes.

WILLIAM MAKEPEACE THACKERAY

A lady's imagination is very rapid;
it jumps from admiration to love,
from love to matrimony in a moment.

JANE AUSTEN

I wish you health – a little wealth
And a happy home with freedom.
And may you always have true friends
But never have cause to need them.

ANON

## THE BEST MAN'S SPEECH

The most popular after-dinner speech on record was made by a man dining with his wife alone in the privacy of their home, and it consisted of one sentence containing seven words of one syllable: "You leave them, dear, I'll do them."

ANON

If men knew how women pass the time when they are alone,
they'd never marry.

O. HENRY (W.S. PORTER)

Wives are young men's mistresses;
companions for middle age; and old men's nurses.

FRANCIS BACON

When a man has married a wife,
he finds out whether
Her knees and elbows are only glued together.

WILLIAM BLAKE

Marriage is an attempt to turn a night owl into a homing pigeon.

ANON

Chumps always make the best husbands. When you marry, Sally, grab a chump. Tap his forehead first, and if it rings solid, don't hesitate. All the unhappy marriages come from husbands having brains. What good are brains to a man? They only unsettle him.

P.G. WODEHOUSE

Spring cleaning is a basic human experience.
Faced in the right, it sets the seal on married love.

PAUL JENNINGS

I ... chose my wife, as she did her wedding gown,
not for a fine glossy surface, but such qualities as
would wear well.

OLIVER GOLDSMITH

## Love

Alas! The love of women! it is known
To be a lovely and a fearful thing.

LORD BYRON

Love makes the world go round.

POPULAR SONG

The course of true love never did run smooth.

WILLIAM SHAKESPEARE

Can love be controlled by advice?

JOHN GAY

Eternal joy, and everlasting love.

THOMAS OTWAY

In the spring a young man's fancy,
Lightly turns to thoughts of love.
O hard, when love and duty clash!

LORD TENNYSON

# THE BEST MAN'S SPEECH

Did you ever hear of Captain Wattle?
He was all for love and a little for the bottle.

CHARLES DIBDIN

I love a lassie.

SIR HARRY LAUDER

Having been in love with one princess or another almost all my life, and I hope I shall go on so, till I die, being firmly persuaded that if I ever do a mean action, it must be in some interval betwixt one passion and another.

LAURENCE STERNE

Let love be without dissimulation.

THE BIBLE

Love is best.

ROBERT BROWNING

Love and murder will out.

WILLIAM CONGREVE

Love is more than gold or great riches.

JOHN LYDGATE

Two souls with but a single thought,
Two hearts that beat as one.

MARIA LOVELL

Women are meant to be loved, not understood.

OSCAR WILDE

And all for love, and nothing for reward.

EDMUND SPENCER

# THE BEST BEST MAN

Of all forms of caution, caution in love is perhaps
the most fatal to true happiness.

BERTRAND RUSSELL

Oh! She was good as she was fair.
None – none on earth above her!
As pure in thought as angels are,
To know her was to love her.

SAMUEL ROGERS

## Various

All women become like their mothers. That is their
tragedy. No man does. That's his.

OSCAR WILDE

A mother's pride, a father's joy!

SIR WALTER SCOTT

Blest is the bride on whom the sun doth shine.

ROBERT HERRICK

Oh Woman, in our hours of ease,
Uncertain, coy and hard to please.

SIR WALTER SCOTT

Why am I always the bridesmaid,
Never the blushing bride?

OLD SONG

A happy bridesmaid makes a happy bride.

LORD TENNYSON

## THE BEST MAN'S SPEECH

I am no orator as Brutus is; but you know me all a plain, blunt man.

WILLIAM SHAKESPEARE

Be sure to leave other men their turns to speak.

FRANCIS BACON

A woman is only a woman,
but a cigar is a good smoke.

RUDYARD KIPLING

Woman will be the last thing civilized by man.

GEORGE MEREDITH

An honest man's the noblest work of God.

ALEXANDER POPE

A wise man makes more opportunities than he finds.

FRANCIS BACON

Apologise to a man if you're wrong,
but to a woman even if you're right.

ANON

An after-dinner speaker is a man who rises to the occasion and then stands too long.

ANON

In public speaking, if you don't strike oil in five minutes, stop boring.

ANON

121

Blessed is the man who having nothing to say, abstains from giving us wordy evidence of the fact.

GEORGE ELIOT

They conquer who think they can.

JOHN DRYDEN

Everything comes to him that hustles while he waits.

THOMAS A. EDISON

Often when we ask for advice we want approval.

ANON

An old man gives good advice in order to console himself for no longer being in a condition to set a bad example.

LA ROCHEFOUCAULD

Men are like fish; neither would get into trouble if they kept their mouths shut.

ANON

## · TELEGRAMS ·

Guests who are unable to attend a wedding should write to the bride's parents expressing regret and perhaps send a gift. A greeting telegram timed to arrive on the wedding day is a good way of conveying best wishes and can be informal. The reading out of wittily composed telegrams can add gaiety to a wedding reception if they are suitable. Telegrams should be vetted prior to their reading and if there are many, it is wise to select a few, otherwise the guests will be quickly bored. All those with the same or similar message such as "Best

# THE BEST MAN'S SPEECH

Wishes" can be grouped together and the greeting mentioned only once. The best man should check with the bride beforehand to find out if there are any which she would specifically like included. Messages should be read clearly with deep breaths taken between each one, allowing everyone the time and opportunity to mutter and exchange comments amongst themselves!

# Checklists

| THE WEDDING PARTY WHO'S WHO |
| --- |
| |
| **BRIDE** |
| **GROOM** |
| **MAID/MATRON OF HONOUR**<br>**(or CHIEF BRIDESMAID)** |
| **BRIDESMAID** |
| **BRIDESMAID** |
| **BRIDESMAID** |
| **PAGE BOY** |
| **PAGE BOY** |
| **PAGE BOY** |
| **BRIDE'S PARENTS** |
| |
| **GROOM'S PARENTS** |
| |

| Name | Address | Tel. No. |
|------|---------|----------|
|      |         |          |
|      |         |          |
|      |         |          |
|      |         |          |
|      |         |          |
|      |         |          |
|      |         |          |
|      |         |          |
|      |         |          |
|      |         |          |
|      |         |          |
|      |         |          |
|      |         |          |

| THE WEDDING PARTY WHO'S WHO | |
|---|---|
| | **Name** |
| **CHIEF USHER** | |
| **USHER** | |
| **USHER** | |
| **USHER** | |

| Address | Tel. No. | Duties, e.g. |
|---|---|---|
| | | **Transport** |
| | | **Escort** |
| | | **Buttonholes** |
| | | **Order of Service Sheets** |

**GUEST LIST
WHO'S WHO**
(For the information of
Best Man and Ushers, e.g.
seating in church and reception)

CHECKLISTS

| DATA FILE |
|---|
| **WEDDING DATE** |

**CEREMONY**

Venue

Arrival time

Officiant

Tel. No.

Fees – when payable

Who will sign the register

Confetti rules

Photo/video restrictions

Parking:    facilities

restrictions

Rehearsal: date

time

get-together venue

---

## DATA FILE

**RECEPTION**

Venue

Contact

Tel. No.

Arrival time

Parking:    facilities

                restrictions

No. of guests

Is a master of ceremonies provided?

If not, what are the arrangements:

   Greeting guests

   Receiving line

   Seating plan

   Grace

   Toastmaster

## DATA FILE

Meal

   Time    –  start

              –  speeches

Bar facilities

Entertainment

Changing room for bride and groom

Departure time for bride and groom

Departure arrangements, e.g. car decorations

Leaving time for guests

**PHOTOGRAPHER**

**Appointed:**

  Name

  Address

  Tel. No.

| DATA FILE |
|---|

**Emergency:**

Name

Address

Tel. No.

**STAG PARTY**

Date

Time

Venue

Transport

# CHECKLISTS

## DATA FILE

**TRANSPORT**

**To church**

Groom & Best Man

Ushers

Guests

**To reception**

Best Man

Ushers

Guests

**To honeymoon**

Bride and Groom

**From reception**

Best Man

Ushers

Guests

## DATA FILE

**Car hire/taxi booked:**

Firm

Address

Tel. No.

Cars to be supplied

Collection/Delivery time

Return time

**Emergency taxi:**

Firm

Address

Tel. No.

CHECKLISTS

| DATA FILE | | |
|---|---|---|
| | **Groom** | **Best Man** |
| | **ATTIRE** | |
| Supplier | | |
| Address | | |
| Tel. No. | | |
| Fitting date | | |
| Collection date | | |
| Alterations date | | |
| Return date (if hired) | | |
| To be returned by whom | | |
| Payment details | | |
| Collection policy | | |

# THE BEST BEST MAN

| DATA FILE | | | | |
|---|---|---|---|---|
| | Groom | | Best Man | |
| | Size | £ | Size | £ |
| Style | | | | |
| Colour | | | | |
| Jacket | | | | |
| Trousers | | | | |
| Waistcoat | | | | |
| Shirt | | | | |
| Tie/cravat | | | | |
| Topper | | | | |
| Gloves | | | | |
| Shoes/socks | | | | |
| Underwear | | | | |
| Handkerchief | | | | |
| Jewellery | | | | |
| Accessories | | | | |
| Buttonholes | | | | |
| TOTAL | | | | |

# DRAFT SPEECH

THE BEST BEST MAN

The morning of the wedding will be busy for the best man as there are some things which cannot be done earlier. It is therefore important to deal with as much as possible prior to the day. This will minimise the rush on the day itself and will do much to calm nerves all round!

| BEST MAN'S DIARY | | |
|---|---|---|
| **Date** | | **Done** |
| | **PREPARATIONS**<br><br>Send written reply immediately on receipt of invitation.<br><br>Purchase wedding gift in consultation with ushers.<br><br>Purchase spare ring.<br><br>Discuss plans with bride, groom and maid/matron of honour (or chief bridesmaid) and make notes.<br><br>Assist the groom with preparations.<br><br>Acquire and pay for own attire in consultation with the bride and groom. | |

| BEST MAN'S DIARY | | |
|---|---|---|
| **Date** | | **Done** |
| | Instruct ushers on their duties and when to perform them. | |
| | Check that the ushers have organised their own attire. | |
| | Arrange transport as necessary. | |
| | Check routes, traffic and timing. | |
| | Prepare and practise speech. | |
| | Check parking arrangements at the church and reception venues. | |
| | Have hair cut. | |
| | Attend rehearsal and present bride and groom with gift. | |
| | Remind groom to acquire all necessary documentation, e.g. licence, passports, traveller's cheques, etc. | |

| BEST MAN'S DIARY | | |
|---|---|---|
| **Date** | | **Done** |
| | Have dress rehearsal with groom. | |
| | Attend stag party and ensure the safety of the groom. | |
| | Check that buttonholes have been ordered. | |
| | Collect order of service sheets and pass on to ushers. | |
| | Collect buttonholes. | |
| | Arrange alarm calls. | |
| | **AFTERWARDS**<br><br>Return hired attire.<br><br>Check security of the newly-weds' home whilst they are on honeymoon.<br><br>Send thank-you note for the bride and groom's gift. | |

| BEST MAN'S DIARY | | |
|---|---|---|
| **Date** | | **Done** |
| | Receive out-of-pocket-expenses repaid by the groom when he returns from honeymoon, unless a sufficient sum has been given to you beforehand to cover all outgoings, in which case you may need to refund the groom!<br><br>Attend entertainment at newly-weds' home when they are settled in, if invited to do so. | |

| USHER'S DIARIES | | |
|---|---|---|
| **Date** | | **Done** |
| | **PREPARATIONS**<br><br>Liaise with best man, devise a timetable and make notes.<br><br>Receive from best man a list of close family to help with seating arrangements in church.<br><br>Acquire attire.<br><br>Have hair cut. | |

A timetable for the wedding day will prepare you for the events to come. The blank timetable at the end of this section may be used to create your own guide.

| **BEST MAN'S TIMETABLE FOR THE DAY** | | |
|---|---|---|
| **Time** | | **Notes** |
| | Rise early.<br>Ring the groom.<br><br>Check with the bride's parents to see if they need any help.<br><br>Pack your own essentials:<br>Cash, emergency telephone numbers, handkerchief(s), umbrellas, speech cards, etc.<br><br>Collect buttonholes and telegrams from bride's mother if not already done.<br><br>Ensure that ushers have order of service sheets and know their duties.<br><br>Ensure that groom's going-away clothes are at the reception venue.<br><br>Ensure that the groom is properly dressed.<br><br>Keep groom calm, smart and prompt.<br><br>Help pack for honeymoon. | |

| BEST MAN'S TIMETABLE FOR THE DAY | | |
|---|---|---|
| **Time** | | **Notes** |
| | Ensure safety of: ring(s); buttonholes; fees, spare cash, foreign currency; travel tickets, traveller's cheques, passports, reservations, driving licence, insurance, banns certificate, inoculation certificates, emergency telephone numbers, umbrella, etc. <br><br>(Ushers should be at the church) <br><br>Accompany groom to church to arrive half an hour before the ceremony is due to start. <br><br>Pay church fees if required to do so before the ceremony. <br><br>Check on ushers. <br><br>Pose for photographs. <br><br>Stand or sit waiting in the front right-hand pew on the right side of and a little behind the groom throughout the ceremony. Sometimes the groom and best man wait in the vestry until a few minutes before the bride is due and then take up their positions. | |

CHECKLISTS

| BEST MAN'S TIMETABLE FOR THE DAY | | |
|---|---|---|
| **Time** | | **Notes** |
| | Take charge of the groom's hat and gloves. | |
| | (Most guests arrive) | |
| | The bride's mother should be the last guest to arrive, signalling to the congregation that the ceremony is about to start. | |
| | The organist changes tempo and begins to play the chosen processional music. | |
| | The ushers stand in the pews at the back of the church. | |
| | The groom and best man rise and move to the head of the aisle; the best man a pace behind the groom. | |
| | The congregation stands. | |
| | The groom and best man may turn to greet the bride as she walks slowly along the aisle or when she arrives at the chancel steps. | |
| | The bride joins the groom. | |

| BEST MAN'S TIMETABLE FOR THE DAY | | |
|---|---|---|
| **Time** | | **Notes** |
| | The bride may turn for the chief bridesmaid to lift her veil and/or to take her bouquets and gloves (if worn).<br><br>The service commences.<br><br>The minister offers the best man the open prayer book onto which you place the ring(s).<br><br>When the minister pronounces the couple man and wife, the best man retreats slightly and to the right-hand side.<br><br>When prompted, escort maid/matron of honour (or chief bridesmaid) to the vestry following the bride and groom. (Offer her your left arm.)<br><br>Sign register if called upon to do so.<br><br>Escort maid/matron of honour (or chief bridesmaid) out of the church following the bride and groom, or: | |

| BEST MAN'S TIMETABLE FOR THE DAY | | |
|---|---|---|
| **Time** | | **Notes** |
| | Stay behind and pay fees (if not already paid). | |
| | Pose for photographs. | |
| | Escort the bride and groom to the first waiting car. They are the first to leave the church grounds. | |
| | Leave for the reception with the maid/matron of honour (or chief bridesmaid) or stay behind to ensure that all guests have transport to the reception if this duty has not been assigned to the chief usher. | |
| | Act as master of ceremonies at the reception if required to do so, although you will not be able to introduce the guests if you have stayed behind at the church. | |

| BEST MAN'S TIMETABLE FOR THE DAY | | |
|---|---|---|
| **Time** | | **Notes** |
| | Join receiving line if you are not acting as master of ceremonies or required to remain behind at the church. | |
| | Mingle with guests. | |
| | Vet the telegrams. | |
| | If acting as master of ceremonies, announce that the meal is about to be served. | |
| | Guide guests to the seating plan and help them to take their places. | |
| | Request silence for grace if previously arranged. | |
| | The meal. | |
| | If acting as master of ceremonies, request silence and call on speakers. | |
| | At the appropriate time, make speech, toast, read any telegrams and messages. | |

| BEST MAN'S TIMETABLE FOR THE DAY | | |
|---|---|---|
| **Time** | | **Notes** |
| | Cake-cutting ceremony. | |
| | Coffee is served. | |
| | The bride and groom lead the dancing. | |
| | Dance with the bride, the maid/matron of honour (or chief bridesmaid), other bridesmaids, mothers of the bride and groom and as many female guests as possible. | |
| | Socialise and rescue the bride and groom from anyone who monopolises their company freeing them to circulate as much as possible. | |
| | Help the groom to change remembering to hand over any documentation. | |
| | Deal with transport and luggage. | |
| | Announce that the couple are about to leave. | |

| BEST MAN'S TIMETABLE FOR THE DAY | | |
|---|---|---|
| **Time** | | **Notes** |
| | Ensure that nothing is left behind by male guests. | |
| | Take charge of groom's clothes. | |
| | Collect gifts. | |
| | Collect a few mementoes. | |
| | Hand telegrams and messages to bride's mother. | |
| | The host, hostess and best man are last to leave. | |
| | Put up your feet and congratulate yourself on a job well done! | |

CHECKLISTS

| USHERS' TIMETABLE FOR THE DAY | | |
|---|---|---|
| **Time** | | **Notes** |
| | Escort bridesmaids during the day.<br><br>Wear buttonhole and distribute to principal wedding party members if necessary.<br><br>Carry umbrellas to shelter guests from inclement weather.<br><br>Collect order of service sheets.<br><br>Arrive at church early (before anyone else).<br><br>Organise car parking.<br><br>Ensure that there are ample order of service sheets at the front of the church for the wedding party.<br><br>Line up on the left side of the church entrance.<br><br>Greet congregation and hand out hymn books, prayer books and/or order of service sheets. | |

| USHERS' TIMETABLE FOR THE DAY | | |
|---|---|---|
| **Time** | | **Notes** |
| | Advise congregation of restrictions regarding photography and/or confetti throwing. | |
| | Offer left arm to females. | |
| | Conduct guests to pews escorting any unescorted lady to her seat:<br><br>   Bride's family and friends on<br>   the left;<br>   Groom's family and friends on<br>   the right. | |
| | Simply escort (without the arm) single men to their seats. | |
| | The first one or two pews at the front of the church should be reserved for close family. The next one or two are for relatives. The groom's parents sit in the second pew from the front. If there are any divorced parents in the families, the ushers should be informed of this by the best man who should explain the relevant seating arrangements. | |

| USHERS' TIMETABLE FOR THE DAY | | |
|---|---|---|
| **Time** | | **Notes** |
| | If the number of guests on each side of the church will clearly be unbalanced, the ushers may use their tact and discretion in filling the seats by positioning guests evenly.<br><br>The last guest to arrive is the bride's mother who should be escorted to her seat by the chief usher to the front pew on the left where she will leave a spare seat on her right for the bride's father (when he has given away the bride).<br><br>Escort any late-comers quietly to pews at the back of the church with minimum fuss and attention so that the service is not disrupted in any way.<br><br>Seat elderly people with walking difficulties near to the aisle and exit.<br><br>As soon as the bride arrives, take own seat at the back ready for the procession. | |

| USHERS' TIMETABLE FOR THE DAY | | |
|---|---|---|
| **Time** | | **Notes** |
| | Service commences followed by the recessional. | |
| | Ensure that all guests have transport to the reception. | |
| | Ensure that the church is left tidy. | |
| | Check that nothing is left behind. | |
| | Offer drinks at the reception. | |
| | Introduce guests to one another. | |
| | Look after bridesmaids. | |
| | Dance with as many guests as possible after other principal members of the wedding party have danced. | |
| | **AFTERWARDS**<br><br>Return hired attire.<br><br>Send thank-you note for gift. | |

# CHECKLISTS

| Time | | Notes |
|------|---|-------|
| | | |

# Index

# INDEX

# INDEX